True Urbanism

Living In and Near the Center

Mark L. Hinshaw, FAICP

PLANNERS PRESS
AMERICAN PLANNING ASSOCIATION
Chicago, Illinois
Washington, D.C.

Copyright 2007 by the American Planning Association
122 S. Michigan Ave., Suite 1600, Chicago, IL 60603

ISBN (paperback edition): 1-932364-27-7 and 978-1-932364-27-9
ISBN (hardbound edition): 1-932364-28-5 and 978-1-932364-28-6

Library of Congress Control Number: 2006940205

Printed in the United States of America

Table of Contents

Acknowledgments

I am greatly indebted to the late William H. Whyte for his inspiration. In 1971, when I was attending graduate school at Hunter College in New York City, "Holly" conducted his path-breaking Street Life Project on the sidewalks of the city—a city which was at that time in its darkest period—and gave me encouragement that urban living could be decent and enriching. I will always treasure Holly's friendship and mentoring, which continued up until his death.

I am also grateful to Neal Peirce, for not only his friendship but his style of writing. Neal has taught me how to discuss complex issues in ways that ordinary readers can grasp. Moreover, Neal's long-standing investigation of urban regions—citistates as he has called them—has inspired me to watch more closely the evolution of cities and their surroundings throughout the country. Neal was one of the first to recognize the growing importance of urban centers in politics, culture, and the economy.

I also wish to acknowledge the late Professor Donald Sullivan, who headed up the Urban Planning program at Hunter College. While I was still a graduate student, Don encouraged me to publish; indeed, he helped me publish a research paper first in a professional journal, which later became a chapter in a book on urban housing. I was Don's research assistant and worked with him to publish his own research. I was greatly saddened by his premature death but continue to remember him fondly.

I must also give due to several editors I have worked with over the years, all of whom helped me advance my research and writing skills. Over the years, both Sylvia Lewis and Ruth Knack at *Planning* magazine have been supportive editors. Bill Thompson at *Landscape Architecture* magazine has given me assignments that have allowed me to observe the changes in many cities right on the streets and within public spaces—places that are important to people.

Susan Cordova has been an unofficial editor for four years, reading all my drafts from the perspective of a lay reader and offering comments and criticisms. Several colleagues deserve recognition for assisting me in the research, sidebars, and graphics for this book. Nathalie Schmidt, Lora Lillard, Sarah Durkee, and Darby Watson all contributed to this work. Sarah helped assemble the images, as well as the Appendix, and Darby wrote one of the chapters.

I wish to also thank the people who offered to read my manuscript. These include Marga Rose Hancocks, Marilee Utter, Michael Stepner, and Tom Eanes. They, along with Neal Peirce, offered numerous insights that have improved the text.

Finally, I wish to thank my children—Erica, Lindsay, and Christopher—for bearing with me for many years. I love you all.

Preface

The Case for True Urbanism

Over the last 15 years, the number, variety, and proliferation of developments planned and designed using principles of new urbanism have been phenomenal. Clearly, the notion of compact, walkable communities appeals to developers, policy makers, and the general public.

The movement has certainly matured well beyond the experimental stage of Seaside and Celebration, two of its early, high-profile, and prototypical communities. It has become more mainstream, finding its way into the plans, policies, and codes of many local municipalities.

Meanwhile, another phenomenon has been taking place during the same period. Although it has not had the benefit of a national organization with a newsletter to sing its praises, it is a movement no less significant and perhaps even holds promise for the future of cities.

LOUIS WIRTH'S URBANISM

In the late 1930s, sociologist Louis Wirth described urbanism as a function of size, density, and heterogeneity. He suggested that the degree of urbanism is shaped by sheer size—that is, major concentrations of people. Furthermore, the number of people located within a given geographic area—i.e. density—drives the degree of urbanity. And the hallmark of true urban places is that they reflect diversity: different ethnicities, races, cultures, age groups, income levels, and so on.

This notion of urbanism, one that is richer and more complex than found in most new urbanist places, is increasingly being found adjacent to the downtowns of major cities across North America. Certainly, older, mature cities such as Boston, New York, and Chicago have had dense urban neighborhoods surrounding their cores for many decades.

What is significant about the current trend is that it is being seen in cities in the western part of the continent that gained prominence in the era of the automobile and suburban expansion. These are communities that meet Wirth's definition. They are large—often consuming several dozens of blocks. They are dense—housing ranges between 80 to 300 units per acre, which is many times more dense than that seen in new urbanist developments. And they are extraordinarily diverse, with a wide range of people, lifestyles, cultures, arts, and commerce.

In a sense, these are places that appeal to folks who prefer walking to driving, who like being around lots of other people, and who enjoy sharing sidewalks and streets, cafes and art galleries, shops and services. They demonstrate the virtues of socially inclusive, collective spaces over private lots and exclusive developments. In contrast to the xenophobic, gated suburban subdivisions predicated on exclusiveness, these urban neighborhoods reflect the unpredictable, ever changing nature of urban living. People who choose to live there embrace diverse people, cultures, and conditions of life, some of which are not always pleasant and photogenic.

It would be highly unlikely for a typical new urbanist community to include, say, a shelter for battered women. Or housing that includes street-level market stalls for Hispanic families to operate businesses out of. Or a gay and lesbian community center. Yet all of these elements of contemporary life can be found in places that exhibit *true* urbanism.

Indeed, when Pyatok Architects begin designing housing developments for close-in neighborhoods, they immediately involve the community to determine how best to meet their needs. This often leads to elements such as space for home-based businesses or extra rooms for extended families. Michael Pyatok is critical of many new urbanist plans that "are picturesque set designs empty of the physical supports that encourage organic or spontaneous economic and social arrangements."

Genuinely urban places appeal to people who are not afraid to live in the 21st century, people who choose exuberantly contemporary buildings over the superficial trappings of 19th century styles—the architectural equivalent of comfort food. These urban dwellers like the energy and vitality of the city, with its widely varied and idiosyncratic qualities.

They are also not afraid of heights. Many Americans seem to have an odd phobia about tall buildings. Many citizens go positively berserk, breaking out the petitions and packing city councils whenever anyone dares to build something taller than several stories. Indeed, many new urbanist plans are careful to stay under five stories lest they spark protracted political battles.

But in places of true urbanism, tall structures are welcome, even celebrated. In these communities, larger buildings allow for many amenities and services, as well as views of water, mountains, or the skyline. In several neighborhoods flanking San Diego's downtown, dozens of new high-rise buildings containing thousands of dwelling units are rising out of an understory of older low-rise structures and parking lots. The towers are architecturally bold and often unashamedly modern—no cloying traditionalism—this is a neighborhood not trying to recreate a romanticized notion of the past; it sees itself firmly rooted in the present.

Moreover, if any word seems to drive many Americans into a state of frenzy, it is the word *density*—as if lots of people living close together were inherently an evil scourge to be prevented at all costs.

Communities emerging next to downtowns recognize the benefits of high density. It simply takes lots of people to support locally owned businesses. Planning policies often promote mixed use and street level retail but then do not allow sufficient densities to provide enough market demand. Hence many developments can only support a handful of national brand stores, such as the ubiquitous Starbucks, Subway, or Hollywood Video, which also require pass-by traffic to survive.

It simply requires lots of people living within a relatively small area to support a complete array of local goods and services. Many citizens bemoan the disappearance of mom-and-pop stores, the neighborhood druggist, or the local movie house, but vigorously lobby their city council to deny new development projects that smack of the "d" word. You can't have it both ways.

In Seattle's Belltown, a relatively new 36-block neighborhood with more than 10,000 residents, the density is sufficiently great to support several specialty bakeries, numerous fine restaurants, drugstores, little markets, many locally owned coffee shops, dry cleaners, unique clothing stores, and businesses offering personal services.

Recently, the number of people now living in Portland's Pearl District justified the opening of a Whole Foods supermarket. Folks in the neighborhood can pick up their daily needs on their walk home from work in the downtown core a few blocks away.

LIVING WITHOUT A CAR

In Belltown, no one worries about bus schedules. Buses travel along most of its streets every five to 10 minutes—not just at peak hours, but throughout the day. Moreover, the buses are free, part of Seattle's downtown-wide service that encourages the use of transit by residents, employees, and shoppers. In Portland's Pearl District, sleek, European-styled streetcars quietly glide down the center of the neighborhood, connecting places where people live to the many things to do in the downtown core.

Some of the people choosing to settle in these places are simply making smart choices for their own lives. Rising gas prices and shrinking petroleum supplies suggest that we should begin looking for ways of living closer to where we work.

Moreover, many people are realizing that at some point we all will, eventually, no longer be able to drive; old age will diminish our faculties. Rather than be stuck out in some isolated, age-restricted, "retirement community" in the desert, these people prefer to live in real neighborhoods, with lots of choices within walking distance.

Several years ago, a Ralph's supermarket was built right on the edge of downtown San Diego, California, in response to the growing number of residents in the adjacent Marina neighborhood, which is packed with new high-rise towers. A new Albertson's market will anchor a mixed use development in the rapidly emerging East Village neighborhood, just east of the downtown's historic Gaslamp Quarter.

For those who occasionally need to drive, other options to owning a vehicle are becoming available. In some cities, a pool of shared automobiles is available. Programs such as Flexcar in Seattle and Zipcar in Washington, D.C., and other cities work something like time-share condominiums. A driver buys a certain number of hours per week. The clean, well-maintained cars are stationed in dozens of convenient locations, available for use even on short notice.

Living in these dense neighborhoods makes many trips by car completely unnecessary. With sufficient density, most goods and services are available within a 10- to -15-minute walk. Indeed, some people are forgoing cars altogether, choosing to spend the $8,000 per year it takes to own, operate, insure, and park a car on other things, such as a larger or more well-appointed place to live. Yes, living in or near a downtown can be more expensive, but it may not be if you deduct the cost of owning a car.

MANY INFLUENCES, DIFFERENT RESULTS, CONSTANT CHANGE

Many new urbanist communities are the product of a single developer and sometimes, only a handful of architects. Most are developed in phases; with each phase fixed in time to offer a pleasant, complete, photogenic quality.

Not so with places exhibiting true urbanism. They are constantly evolving, infilling, and redeveloping, and have a broad mixture of architectural styles and sensibilities. They reflect Richard Sennett's notion of the "Uses of Disorder." They have a gritty urbanity that values variety over uniformity. Rarely are they subject to a highly prescriptive set of design standards; rather, they thrive with the idea that everything need not fit an ideal. They may be subject to design guidelines and a design review process, but those techniques encourage creativity over conformity.

Such places—like all real cities—are continually in transition. They are subject to successions of different people, businesses, and types of buildings. Their character cannot easily be captured in still photographs, as it is dynamic and ever changing. Indeed, Jason Luker of the San Diego Centre City Development Corporation notes that his agency's illustrated bulletin describing the neighborhood can't keep up with the changes.

And these neighborhoods embrace different social needs. They differ from earlier examples of rapidly transformed urban neighborhoods like SoHo in New York, which saw gentrification push out the initial people who "pioneered" living there. In San Diego, an aggressive program to build attractive single room occupancy (SRO) housing has ensured that many lower income individuals can continue to be a part of the downtown community. In Seattle, numerous nonprofits, aided by tax credits, state housing funds, and a taxpayer-approved low-income housing levy, have built or renovated thousands of units.

As true urbanist communities develop, they are shaped by scores—perhaps hundreds—of people. They emerge from the collective decisions of many organizations, associations, corporations, and government bodies, not from a single vision. They value the results of democracy—however messy, unpredictable, and uneven they may be.

ATTRACTING THE CREATIVE CLASS

Richard Florida has observed that certain cities, and certain neighborhoods within them, tend to attract people who are extraordinarily creative in their professional lives. These are people active in the arts, technology, information, research, and communication—all elements that drive major sectors of our culture and economy.

Such people find denser, more diverse places appealing because they embody a high tolerance for different ideas, expressions, behavior, lifestyles, and sexual preferences. They offer a milieu of energy and entrepreneurialism. While creative people can be fiercely independent, they also value the collective social life of streets, cafes, and public spaces, and the proximity of many different people.

It is hard to imagine many people of Florida's creative class choosing the places touted by new urbanists, such as Celebration. They are simply not dense or diverse enough to support a broadly creative culture.

Belltown in Seattle, the Golden Triangle in Denver, the Pearl District in Portland, and the East Village in San Diego all have the same proximity to arts, culture, entertainment, and nightlife. Such access to a wide range of choices comes only with the intensities and densities found in urban centers.

Many of these dense, close-in neighborhoods are attracting creative people from other countries, who are used to living in cities. Their families are unbound by the uniquely American notion that families require single-family houses. These folks know that is nonsense, and that kids can be raised perfectly well in the middle of the city.

All around the edges of Vancouver, British Columbia's central core are dense, high-rise neighborhoods containing families with children. Through its policies and its investments, Vancouver makes sure that these neighborhoods have schools, parks, and community centers. American cities used to do the same thing. But in the last several decades, investments in such public goods have tended to be in outlying neighborhoods, not near the centers.

NOT JUST BIG CITIES

If the phenomenon of a dramatic increase in downtown living were just being seen in a few, high-profile, "hip" coastal cities, it might be dismissed as a limited and short-lived trend. But such places are cropping up in all sorts of unexpected locations. Dense new downtown neighborhoods are emerging in cities like Oakland and Long Beach, California, and Tacoma, Washington. Even cities deep in the American heartland like St. Paul, Minnesota; Kansas City, Missouri; and Dallas are seeing aspects of this trend.

Older suburbs that are now becoming cities in their own right are also seeing a similar change. Stamford, Connecticut; Bethesda, Maryland; Bellevue, Washington; Walnut Creek; and Pasadena, California, are seeing thousands of units of dense housing built next to their commercial cores, something that was unthinkable 10 or 15 years ago.

INVESTMENTS, INCENTIVES, AND INTERVENTIONS

This breathtakingly fast move toward truly urban living has not come without considerable public sector involvement.

San Diego's redevelopment agency has been very aggressive in acquiring and assembling land, and tax increment funds have been used to improve infrastructure as well as finance affordable units. According to Michael Stepner, FAICP, this has prevented the gentrification that has occurred in other cities in the past and ensures that the new neighborhoods contain a wide variety of people.

Stepner also notes the important role of government in "priming the pump." "By having the city stimulate initial housing developments," he observes, "the entire image of the downtown was altered. People began to perceive it as a viable place to live."

Portland built a new streetcar line to serve the burgeoning neighborhoods northwest of the downtown core. Sleekly modern streetcars loop around the dense configuration of residential and mixed use developments in the Pearl District. Similarly, in San Diego bright red trolleys serve a number of stops in the new urban neighborhoods that surround the downtown core.

Sometimes change can be fueled by regulatory changes that open up new opportunities for private investment. Seattle rezoned the north part of its downtown in the '80s to limit the amount of commercial development allowed and vastly increase the amount of allowable residential development. This was coupled with a change to the building code that allowed a form of mid-rise, light-frame construction considerably less costly than concrete or steel. Since then, thousands of units have been constructed in Belltown.

Portland's Development Commission has sponsored numerous high-quality projects throughout downtown and has invested in parks and streetscape improvements. The recently opened Jamison Square, with a unique water fountain that is popular with children, forms a sort of village green in the center of the Pearl District.

Places that exhibit the qualities of true urbanism—density, diversity, energy, and sociability—offer enormous promise for American cities. No longer are downtowns just places of commerce, culture, spectator sports, and entertainment. They are becoming terrific places to live.

1

Demography, Density, and Diversity

The next 40 years will be unlike anything our culture and our country have seen in the past. Our demographic composition is changing dramatically. Technology is offering both new opportunities and new problems. Economic forces—international, national, regional, and local—are transforming rapidly. And we have no idea now what all of the ramifications will be.

No longer are our economy and society fueled by expanding families. The number of households is rapidly rising, but the size of those households is falling. The last five decades have been marked by an outward expansion across the landscape by families in search of the American Dream of a large, freestanding house on a large lot. While it has not altogether disappeared, that singular dream is being supplanted by a myriad of other preferences.

Just as elementary schools were dramatically affected by the baby boom generation in the '50s, and colleges were affected in the '60s and '70s, the aging of this demographic group will have enormous consequences for all of our public institutions. Just as the composition and character of the workplace was dramatically altered by this same population cohort in the '80s and '90s, this change will cause us to seek new directions in the delivery of goods and services, health care, forms of transportation, recreation, and many other aspects of our society. We will see new institutional structures, new forms of employment, and perhaps different types of government.

The next several decades will see fundamental shifts in many aspects of the culture, the economy, and the physical environment. And what is now just building as a wave will be upon us with the force of a tsunami. In the coming decades, we will see this manifested in our communities, our neighborhoods, and our housing stock and how it is configured and combined with other uses and functions. We have a whole new set of expectations and demands being formed by a different makeup of our population.

THE NEW AMERICAN FAMILY

For some time, we Americans have held on to a notion of the typical family: two adults with two children. That ideal—the nuclear family— is rapidly diminishing. Less than 25 percent of households now fit that type.

Take a look at Figure 1-1. For several decades now the number of people per household has steadily declined, while the number of households has steadily increased. Census data indicates that the fastest growing segments of our society fall within one of these groups: singles,

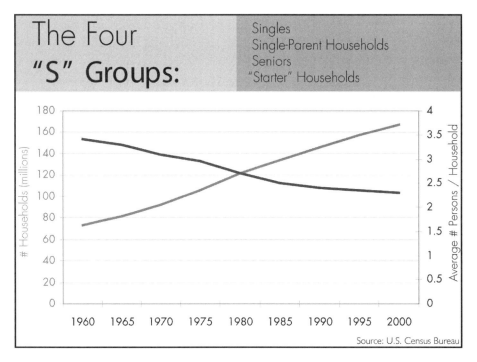

Fig. 1-1. This graph illustrates the decrease in the size of households occurring at the same time as the number of households has increased.

single-parent households, seniors, or "start-up" households—that is, young couples, whether married or unmarried, straight or gay.

These groups now make up at least half the population. In another 10 years or so, they will approach 60 percent of the population. In recent surveys, relatively few of these people have preferences for places to live that match those of previous generations. They are looking for types of homes and types of neighborhoods that are entirely different.

Let's take a look at one segment—seniors.

Right now, people over 60 years old constitute 15 to 16 percent of our population—approximately one in seven. In another 15 years, as the baby boom generation ages, this will grow to between 20 and 25 percent—close to one in four.

Now consider Figure 1-2. We are simply living longer. Because of better nutrition, exercise, preventative medicine, curative medicine, cleaner air and water, and a host of other reasons, we have almost doubled longevity from what it was a century ago. Not long ago, it was

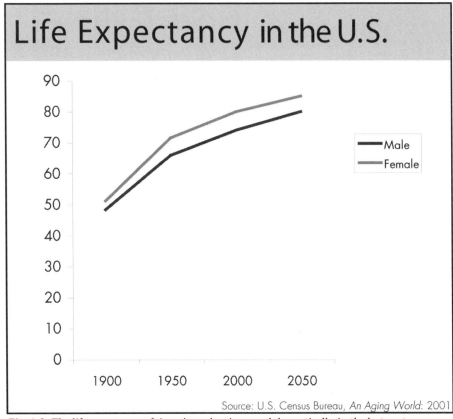

Fig. 1-2. The life expectancy of Americans has increased dramatically in the last century.

very uncommon for people to live into their 90s. Not anymore. Both men and women can expect to live long lives, perhaps 20 to 30 years past what we have traditionally considered to be retirement age.

But now look at Figure 1-3. Although we may be living longer, our faculties, such as visual acuity, hand-eye coordination, and responsiveness, still decline. Fatalities attributed to drivers over age 70 go up exponentially. (There is a corresponding set of data for drivers under 20, but that is a different story.) At some point, insurance companies will no longer tolerate paying out big claims in these cases and will force people to relinquish their driver's licenses. Even now, many elderly people have their licenses revoked by testing agencies when they fail their renewal exams. Simply because of this growing number of accidents and road deaths, some states might start setting a maximum driving age.

Whatever the reason, more elderly people will simply find themselves with no personal access to an automobile. Just as we have no such

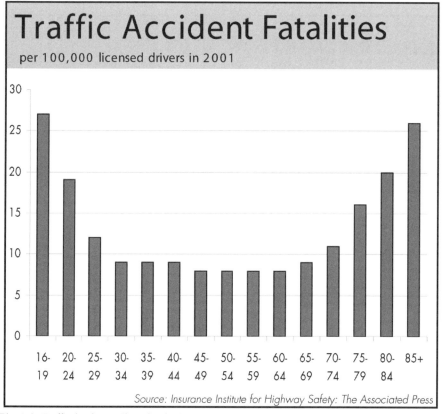

Fig. 1-3. Traffic deaths attributed to both younger and older drivers are significantly greater than to age groups in between.

access during the first 15 years of our lives, we may be in the same state for the last 15. Some people realize this and even now seek choices in locations and forms of living that will enable them to be independent.

I believe that few people in the baby boom group will find it acceptable to be "warehoused" in retirement centers, especially those tucked away in remote locations. This segregation of our most senior people is debilitating and insulting and forces dependency on corporate or institutional caregivers. The emerging generation of elderly people will by far prefer to live in real communities, in real neighborhoods, on real streets—with many, many choices of services, entertainment, and culture close at hand. People will want to be surrounded by arts and culture, lively parks, public spaces, recreation, shopping, and health care.

People will begin to consider what they will need to have within a reasonably short walking distance of their homes. Some very sharp and prescient people are already engaged such personal planning. The impact this alone will have on restructuring communities is enormous.

Consider this as well: Some people are *not* retiring, at least in the conventional sense of ceasing to be employed. They might officially retire from one job but soon take another, perhaps working part time. We already see this in certain service businesses where a few decades ago positions filled by teenagers are now taken by seniors. And employers like this trend. Seniors are responsible, stable, savvy, sensitive to customers, and stay loyal to a company.

As journalist Bob Moos noted in "Go for the Golden" in the November 20, 2005, *Dallas Morning News*, certain employers such as Radio Shack are hiring older workers "because they know how to relate to customers, have a strong work ethic, and are role models for younger employees." A spokesman for Radio Shack was quoted as saying, "Older adults know how to get the job done."

But if seniors are faced with less automobile-related mobility, they will increasingly choose places to live where they can walk to work or use public transportation to reach the job. It is unlikely that elderly people will tolerate the long, exhausting commutes they might have endured earlier in their lives.

So what we now have is a fascinating—perhaps unprecedented—convergence of values between widely different age groups, a phenomenon not seen before in American society. People who are relatively young and people who are relatively old prefer to live in places that are lively, offer many choices, and are packed with arts, culture, and entertainment. Already, the many espresso bars and bistros that are popping up in our cities appeal to both the young and the old. These "Third

Places," as Ray Oldenberg identified them, are valued by many people for their sociability and casual atmosphere. We may soon see the rise of English pub-like places that combine food, drink, and camaraderie.

There is already an interesting version of this occurring in some quarters. Developer Ron Sher in Seattle has discovered that he can provide places for people to hang out while providing goods and services. His Third Place Books store, which anchors the town center of Lake Forest Park north of Seattle, offers a comfortable setting in which to buy and read books. Its library-like arrangement of tables and chairs and overstuffed sofas is surrounded by kiosks of vendors selling coffee and inexpensive meals. People start arriving at 7 a.m. and the place stays busy

Fig. 1-4. Pioneer Courthouse Square in downtown Portland appeals to all ages both day and night. Source: Walker Macy Landscape Architects.

until midnight. I suspect he could keep the place open 24 hours a day if he chose to.

Clearly, people of widely varying ages see the value of spending time in social settings. Perhaps we are simply getting weary of the low-grade, uninspired twaddle that has been dished out for too many years on television. Many people yearn for the stimulation found in public places.

An interesting barometer of this change is found in Pioneer Courthouse Square in the middle of downtown Portland, Oregon. On some nights, 20-somethings lounge about listening to the music of local rock bands. On other evenings, decked-out seniors can be seen square dancing late into the night. We are beginning to relearn the pleasures of enjoying one another's company in the public realm. We need not escape the city; indeed, we are embracing it.

DENSITY AS DESTINY

Since the early 1950s, Americans have viewed density as something like a four-letter word. This attitude might have had a rightful origin in previous patterns of urban development in which big cities were marked first by block after block of crowded tenements and later, by repetitive public housing complexes. Indeed, much planning and public health literature of the early 20th century dwelled upon conditions of "over-crowding" in cities. Even in mid-century, it was popular for writers to cite the Calhoun rat experiment as evidence that people living close together would cause social disorder, crime, and even murderous behavior.

Such cynical observations reached their zenith at the same time as many American cities experienced record incidents of criminal acts, deterioration of public infrastructure, and graffiti run amok on buildings, transit vehicles, and bridge structures. So imbedded in many people's minds was urban disintegration that even years after New York City's subway system found a paint that prevented the adherence of graffiti, Hollywood persisted in showing city scenes of people riding in cars covered with wild and obscene scrawls.

Indeed, so much American mythology has been focused upon the supposed evils of the city and the degradation of the lower classes when packed into hovels that it took until the early '60s and Jane Jacobs's path-breaking book, *The Death and Life of Great American Cities*, to begin to dispel the notion of density as undesirable. Even now, many citizens equate even moderate density development with crime and drugs.

So powerful was the idea that density was to be purged from urban areas that many cities literally eviscerated themselves by clearing away large sections of housing. American culture has had a persistent strain of antiurbanism that may reach back to our Puritan roots, when public life was full of strictures to fight the temptations to sin that lurked around every corner.

Although it is questionable whether there was actually any deliberate national policy to thin density and depopulate cities, the effect of the

---

Picket Fence to Skyline View
By Motoro Rich

For decades, home builders have fed the seemingly endless appetite for the suburban four-bedroom house with the backyard and the picket fence. But increasingly, they are recasting the American dream as a two-bedroom condominium with a gym in the basement and a skyline view from the living room.

Some of the biggest names in suburban home building are getting into urban condominium development or greatly expanding their presence there. In the New York metropolitan area, urban condos now represent nearly a third of sales for K. Hovnanian Homes, a national suburban home builder based in Edison, N.J., up from 5 percent five years ago. KB Home, a national developer that has built more than 146,000 homes in suburban subdivisions in the last five years, launched a new urban division last year, which is now building its first project, 200 condo units on top of a hotel in downtown Los Angeles.

At WCI Communities, a Florida-based builder that sold 1,900 single-family homes last year, high-rise development has risen to 40 percent of the company's sales last year from 27 percent of sales in 2000. And in the Bay Area of California, fully half of the sales at Pulte Homes, the nation's second-largest home builder, come from urban condos and town houses, up from none five years ago. The business decision represented by these moves may reflect a major social shift, in which, after two decades of rezoning, promoting and hoping on the part of city governments and urban planners, cities are finally becoming attractive again for large numbers of middle class residents. "The suburbs are overbuilt, crowded and continuing to spread, and the commutes are getting longer," said John K. McIlwain, a senior resident fellow for housing at the Urban Land Institute, a nonprofit research group. Meanwhile, "cities are actually much cleaner, healthier and better run than they were 20 years ago."

Fig. 1-5. The River North District in downtown Chicago was one of the first close-in neighbor-hoods in the country to see a dramatic increase in housing, beginning in the 1990s. Since then many other cities have witnessed a similar phenomenon. Source: Sylvia Lewis.

National Defense Highway Act—which created the interstate system of freeways—coupled with low-interest Veterans Administration and Federal Housing Authority home loans and tax deductible mortgage interest, did just that. Many middle-class citizens who decry "social engineering" do not seem to realize that these programs were immense and unprecedented methods of inducing specific behavior.

But now, 50 years later, several generations of antiurban biases are crumbling. So swift has the sea-change occurred that in some places it has been almost breathtaking. Certain "first-tier" cities have seen entire neighborhoods surrounding the downtown transformed in barely more than a decade. Places like River North in Chicago, Lower Downtown in Denver, and the Pearl District in Portland are now filled with renovated and new buildings containing higher density housing. But in big cities, such change might have been expected. Less known are the many smaller communities where similar transformations are taking place.

For example, Springfield, Missouri, once a railroad town dotted with grain elevators and stockyards, saw its downtown decline during the

Fig. 1-6. Although it is squarely in the American heartland, Springfield, Missouri, is also seeing a great interest in downtown living. Source: LMN Architects.

'70s and '80s to the point where empty department stores, vast parking lots, and abandoned rail lines became its new identity. In the last several years, however, the place is packed with locally owned restaurants, cafes, coffee bars, night spots, and specialty shops. Developers cannot convert Victorian-era buildings into lofts fast enough to meet the demand. Even new loft buildings are being planned.

This "rediscovery of the center" was noted early by the late William H. "Holly" Whyte in his prescient book, *City*. But Holly did not foresee the spectacular increase in the role of arts and culture in central cities, a demand that is strongly associated with the people who are choosing downtown neighborhoods rather than suburbs.

Density now may be seen as positively correlated with a city's cultural and artistic status, not merely with its financial stature. Those cities with increasingly strong and vibrant economies, as well as flourishing arenas of education and arts, are precisely those that are seeing high density development. So the cycle has begun to come full circle. Density is again seen as beneficial, appealing, and in demand.

And this increasingly dynamic trend differs from previous "back to the city" movements that resulted in gentrification in decades past. The rebirth of neighborhoods like SoHo in New York, Adams-Morgan in Washington, D.C., and Beacon Hill in Boston essentially involved a rapid succession of populations. Early "urban pioneers," whether artists or minorities, were eventually pushed out by rising rents and property values.

Now, new or rediscovered inner city neighborhoods are home to people with a wide array of incomes, ethnicities, and lifestyles. Often this new urban soup is rich with different flavors, marked as it is by different languages, cultures, and values. It is not uncommon for streets to be filled with people chattering away in foreign tongues or running restaurants of exotic origins, from Cuban to African to Indian. It is clear that close-in districts are once again welcoming people from countries and cultures all over the world as they have done in the past. We are rediscovering not only the virtues of density, but of diversity as well.

REFERENCES

Moos, Bob. "Go for the Golden," *Dallas Morning News*, November 20, 2005.

Oldenberg, Ray. 1991. *The Great Good Place*. New York: Paragon House.

Jacobs, Jane. 1961. *The Death and Life of Great American Cities*.

Whyte, William H. 1988. *City: Rediscovering the Center*. New York: Doubleday.

2

Different Cultures, Different Values

I live in a 27-story building in the heart of Seattle's Belltown. I am white, but am surrounded by people from different places in the world with different incomes and different lifestyles. For example ...

My tailor is a sharp, affable, and amusing Korean woman. She runs a shop that sells and rents clothing for weddings and other social functions that demand formal attire. Her dog, a small pug, sits by the door on a pillow and greets each customer with a drooling grin. Katie Chun works hard, often putting in 12-hour days. She's a fixture on the street and seems to know everyone. Once, when I desperately needed a tux shirt repaired on short notice, she offered to do it and bring it up to my apartment that same evening.

Next door to her shop is a French bakery, managed by Gregoire, who grew up in Brittany. The doors to the bakery are flung open in the early morning hours to let in some cool air. I always look forward to getting an early morning cab to the airport just for the chance to breathe in that sweet smell of freshly baked bread. Folks in the neighborhood hang out for hours at the little Parisian-style tables. A couple of years ago, a young female cashier who worked there fell in love with the gregarious doorman. They both disappeared shortly thereafter.

Around the corner, a Cambodian family operates a dollar store in an older building. I can be assured that if I need a household item that is somewhat obscure—say, for instance, disposable bamboo skewers—they will likely have it. I suspect they make their money mainly by selling tobacco products and lottery tickets, neither of which I purchase,

Fig. 2-1. Small, locally owned cafes, like the Nantaise Bakery in Seattle, have become popular hangouts in many urban neighborhoods. They allow people to feel they're in a small town while living in a larger city. Source: Mark Hinshaw.

but I am pleased that other people's addictive habits allow me to have such a store within a five-minute stroll.

A few blocks away, an East Indian woman manages a Chinese restaurant. Once when I was ill, she personally delivered a meal right to my home. She even stayed awhile to keep me company and we chatted about her business. Thousands of new area residents have made it so successful that the cafe recently expanded into a full-service restaurant with an upscale lounge featuring live, late-night jazz.

On the corner is a pan-Asian restaurant owned by a Thai family. They know me by my first name and start preparing my favorite dish as I walk in the door. The staff is a mix of family members and other young people who come and go. The chef nods and smiles to me amid an almost constant ballet of swirling woks, tossed vegetables, and steaming cauldrons of soup and rice.

Not far from where I live, there is a little cafe that specializes in crepes—not unlike the tiny establishments found throughout Paris. The couple that owns it is from Bosnia. Their personal history is filled with the tragedies of war and ethnic strife. But they clearly love what they do and grin broadly while chatting with customers and putting out some splendid meals wrapped in thin, hot, rapidly cooked dough.

The list goes on. The hair salon a block away is owned by a loquacious Hispanic woman. An exotic import shop a few blocks south is run by a man from Nigeria. The neighborhood Rite Aid pharmacy is staffed by people of different races and ethnicities. While we don't (yet) have a supermarket within walking distance, we have something far better: Pike Place Market, a huge aggregation of one-of-a-kind food vendors, specialty shops, cafes, fish mongers, and purveyors of fruits and vegetables. Each business is owned or managed by someone from one of so many different nationalities that the list would run to pages. The luscious

Fig. 2-2. Multiethnic commerce has enriched the vitality of many close-in neighborhoods, such as Little Saigon in Seattle. Source: Mark Hinshaw.

bouquet of flowers perched on my table was grown, picked, and artfully arranged by an extended family of Hmong immigrants.

Every morning in the Uptown Espresso coffee shop across the street, a middle-aged African American man quietly goes through a ritual. He plops in to the same wingback armchair and unpacks a small chessboard from his backpack. He lays out the little game board and slowly sets up the pieces. He then takes out a thick manual of chess moves and methodically recreates strategies, pausing to jot notes in the margins of the book. His large paper cup of coffee must last him through numerous tutorials, as he is there when I enter and he is still there when I leave 40 minutes later.

The elevator in my building sometimes seems like a small meeting room in the United Nations. I hear Chinese, Japanese, Russian, French, German, Polish, Spanish … even some languages I cannot decipher. Some of these folks have families with young children.

Take Djaimi and Matthew, my neighbors on the sixth floor. She is French; Matthew is Australian. They have lived all over the world and, for now, are in Seattle. They have two young girls who are quite fearless when it comes to living right in the center of the city. They take swimming classes in the building's pool and chalk hopscotch patterns on the sidewalk. The bakery gives the girls cookies and the dogs in the neighborhood are overjoyed to see humans close to their size. This family doesn't care about the typical middle-class "American lifestyle" of a house in the suburbs. They know perfectly well that it is possible to raise a family squarely in the center of the city.

The propensity that downtowns have for accommodating cultural diversity has been noted by Eugenie Birch, FAICP, of the University of Pennsylvania. She has researched demographic changes in the downtowns of more than 40 cities over a 30-year period. Professor Birch found that downtowns are more diverse than the population of the nation as a whole, and certainly more diverse than suburban communities.

In an article heralding the rebirth of the South Bronx (or SoBro as it is now called in some quarters), the *New York Times* noted in an article on June 24, 2005, that people moving into the district were attracted to "the allures of the long-standing Latino and African American culture—sidewalk dominoes games, flamboyant murals, lush, vacant-lot gardens and restaurants with fried plantains and mango shakes—that give the neighborhood a populist authenticity …"

People who choose to live downtown do so, in part at least, because it offers a slice of the world at your doorstep. Contrary to what some people believe, living amidst high density is not alienating or impersonal; indeed, it is both intimate and sociable. Downtowns by nature embody the collective energy of many very different people. While many suburbs were founded on a kind of xenophobia—a fear of strangers—downtown living revels in it. Being exposed to so many different people on a daily basis encourages tolerance for other cultures, choices, or preferences.

Living in a densely populated area also changes one's perspective with regard to the sense of community. Rather than just protecting their personal property, residents nurture the neighborhood as a whole. Shopkeepers sweep the sidewalks and put out flowerpots. Residents stroll about with their dogs in tow. Visitors are welcome but are monitored by numerous "eyes on the street." The maintenance people in our building trim the hedges along the curb and pick up trash. The local coffee shop hosts political action groups and social events. Occasionally, runners for charity functions flood the streets. And people come out of the park on our block on their way to one of the numerous restaurants or nightspots that are found throughout the district.

In other words, the attitude is about welcoming many different people *in* rather than finding ways to keep them *out*. It's a fundamentally different state of mind than is found, unfortunately, in many North American communities. One could call it a "liberal" perspective. Perhaps that is why, nationally, "blue precincts" fairly closely coincide with census districts with higher densities. This correlation was identified by the Seattle alternative weekly newspaper *The Stranger* in the weeks following the 2004 national election. The editors dubbed this congruence of density and political leaning the "urban archipelago" or "The United Cities of America."

It might be easy for some to dismiss this phenomenon of people choosing to live in or close to downtowns as something found in only a handful of bigger cities on the coasts. But the same thing, albeit on a smaller scale, is happening in many places, even in the heartland. Dallas, Indianapolis, Minneapolis, and Kansas City all have city centers with similar diversity. But so do much smaller communities. In-town living is also taking place where there is a compact form of development with denser housing available within close proximity to the center. It is being seen in Washougal, Washington (population 10,000), and in Springfield, Missouri (pop. 150,000). So it is in Coeur d'Alene, Idaho (pop. 40,000), and in Fresno, California (pop. 450,000). It happens wherever there is a deliberate attempt to reenergize a downtown by opening up places to live.

HOUSING FOR EVERYONE

Not too many years ago, Long Beach, California, was languishing. Headquarters of the largest port on the West Coast, it was a community with a vacant downtown. As with many older cities, when the department stores moved out, many other local businesses could not survive and closed. Office buildings emptied out, hotels turned into flophouses, and the streets became havens for robbery, assault, drug trafficking, and other crimes.

But in the past 10 years, downtown Long Beach has almost entirely turned around. A new shopping district has housing on its upper floors. A multiscreen cinema attracts people well into the evening. (The district even includes an urban Wal-Mart, its big box tamed to fit graciously as the backdrop to a public square.) This development did not follow the standard model of an enclosed mall, an earlier trend that exacerbated the vacant atmospheres of many downtowns. Rather, buildings line streets that extend the grid of the city. Nearby, sidewalks are lined with dozens of restaurants and nightspots.

This is a city in which 36 percent of the population is Hispanic. At times, Long Beach feels like the capital city of a Latin American country. But Long Beach is home to wide range of people. One entire neighborhood is primarily Cambodian.

But perhaps one of the most remarkable districts in Long Beach is the neighborhood just to the east of downtown. Several years ago, gay and

Fig. 2-3. A recently built housing development in Oakland, California, includes commercial spaces along the sidewalk to accommodate businesses owned by Hispanic families. Source: Pyatok and Associates, Architects.

lesbian couples in Los Angeles discovered homes were considerably less expensive in this area. They started snapping up little Craftsman houses, bungalows, and beach cabins and set to renovating them. Then they started investing in shops, services, galleries, cafes, and coffee houses. The result is a neighborhood that hums with idiosyncratic energy. Gardens are lush and porches face onto gracious, tree-lined streets.

Left to its own devices, the market will often push out the very people who initially invested their own sweat and equity into a reviving neighborhood. The classic case is SoHo in New York.

In the early 1970s SoHo did not exist. The district was merely a collection of decrepit warehouses with grimy cast-iron facades. The city had decided to allow working artists to live there and occasionally, one could see brass plaques next to doors with the initials A.I.R.—artist in residence. This was done to inform firefighters that there were people in the building, not just materials.

But as is now the stuff of legend, the struggling artists were first shoved aside by very successful artists, who were in turn displaced by stockbrokers and attorneys. Despite the presence of numerous art galleries, today relatively few artists can afford to live in SoHo.

A free-market economist might say, "It's a cold, cruel world—a sort of economic Darwinism." I even once heard someone from this perspective cynically declare his version of the Golden Rule: "Whoever has the gold makes the rules." This callous and grasping attitude has given rise to a notion that in cities, newcomers are a bad thing.

Indeed, many people decry the gentrification of central city neighborhoods as if the alternative of disinvestment and deterioration were somehow preferable. Some cities are working very hard to ensure that this "inevitable" process of displacement does not occur. But it does require some degree of intervention in the normal marketplace.

San Diego SROs

For the past 20 years, San Diego, through its Centre City Development Corporation, has promoted Single Room Occupancy (SRO) housing as a means of getting people off the street. By all counts it has been a wildly successful program. While it is still possible to see homeless people on downtown sidewalks, their presence is much less compared with that in many other cities.

Homeless people are an "at-risk" population group. They can be robbed, raped, and beaten and fall prey to drug dealers. They easily get sick, picking up illnesses from alleys, dumpsters, and sleeping outside.

Some freeze to death during winters. Others are hit by vehicles. San Diego gets these people into safe and clean shelters, but not the typical "shelters" many cities are accustomed to. I certainly do not mean to denigrate faith-based organizations and nonprofits that play an important role in addressing the homeless problem by providing shelters. But often these places are not open around the clock, and people line downtown sidewalks or camp out as they wait for the shelters to open.

Throughout downtown San Diego there are numerous well-designed apartment buildings containing very small units. Residents share bathrooms and have common kitchen and recreation areas. Some of these are arranged around landscaped courtyards and all are managed by full-time staff, who monitor behavior and visitors. The living spaces are small, but the rents are very low—low enough that people on assistance can afford them. Some residents are relatively independent, holding part-time or minimum wage jobs.

According to Michael Stepner, FAICP, former city architect for San Diego, the city opened the door to the creation of new SRO units by changing its building codes. "Toilets could be located next to the

Fig. 2-4. Scattered throughout downtown San Diego are several new single-room-occupancy apartment buildings that house low income individuals in pleasant, safe, and supervised settings. Source: Mark Hinshaw.

Compact Living Units (CLUs) in San Diego

Between 1970 and 1985, more than 1,200 SRO units were demolished within and around downtown San Diego. The gentrification of the old Gaslight District downtown led to further concerns over a potential increase in the homeless population. Initially, the city responded by requiring that developers replace any SROs that would be demolished. However, below-market rental rates for SROs were insufficient to cover costs of building. Furthermore, SROs were considered too small for permanent accommodations, and a full stu-

dio in San Diego was still more than many people could afford. This policy expired after three years, and city officials decided instead to make changes to its codes. A new type of dwelling unit was designated and legalized: the Compact Living Unit (CLU). Incentives from the city included low-interest financing, an expansion of the areas where the units would be allowed, few or no parking requirements, reduced water and sewer fees, and, finally, an expedited permit review process.

---

kitchen sink, but separated by a partition. An outlet and small counter for a microwave was also allowed," he explains. "We made these changes not only for tenants who desired more privacy than was offered by communal kitchens and baths, but for building operators, who often had problems with clogged drains because tenants used in-room sinks for food preparation. Smuggled-in hot plates and toaster ovens would be placed on beds, causing fires." Such simple, common-sense fixes to outdated codes are often necessary.

Many of the SRO buildings were designed by Rob Quigley, a very creative local architect who has taken on social issues as a personal cause. His buildings have a sense of style, sometimes even a quirkiness that infuses these modest places with a high degree of dignity. Some are so well designed—even on very constrained budgets—that they could easily be mistaken for market-rate rentals. Several buildings contain ground-level shops and services oriented both to the residents as well as to the general public. I suspect that some people dining at one of the chic cafes have no idea that they are surrounded by formerly homeless individuals.

Seattle Nonprofits

In 2005, the Downtown Seattle Association (DSA) celebrated the 25th year of a successful spin-off organization, the Housing Resources

Group (HRG). Back in the early '80s, several prominent business leaders were prompted by Virginia Anderson, a downtown leader and aggressive housing advocate, to create a means by which to build housing for the people of very modest incomes.

Anderson argued that many of these people worked in the downtown area. They were cooks, waiters, janitors, security people, and many others who contributed quietly to making downtown function. They often had such modest incomes that they did not own cars and used transit to get to work. Her assertion was that they should have an opportunity to live near where they worked.

Her argument convinced downtown corporations, banks, and developers and they have since then contributed many millions of dollars to the HRG. It combined private contributions with low-income tax credits, syndications, and state housing funds to build dozens of high-quality apartment buildings. Over 2,000 units have been constructed. HRG not only ensures that the buildings are designed well, but they guarantee their longevity through very professional management and ongoing maintenance. Consequently, HRG projects look as clean and crisp today as when they were first built.

Fig. 2-5. The Gilmore is one of many low-income housing developments developed by a nonprofit spin-off of the Downtown Seattle Association. Source: Mark Hinshaw.

Jane Hampton lives in the Vine Court, one of the early HRG buildings. It sits squarely in the middle of what is now the "hot" real estate of Seattle's Belltown. The street is lined with cafes and coffeehouses, bodegas and bakeries, chic hair salons, and trendy clothing stores. Jane works at a Starbucks serving espresso drinks, and before that she was a clerk at one of the Rite Aids downtown, a few blocks from her place. Jane is an attractive, middle-aged African American woman who likes to occasionally dress up flamboyantly and go out on the town. Many people in the neighborhood know her for her affable nature and colorful attire. Jane is one of the many unique individuals who make Belltown an interesting place to live.

Jane's is not the only HRG building on First Avenue. Several others dot the street, most occupying gracious brick facades that do not reveal that they contain lower income housing. Some even have upscale restaurants, art galleries, and nightclubs.

And HRG is not the only nonprofit that builds and manages housing for lower income people in downtown. The Plymouth Housing Group was the 2005 recipient of the Downtown Seattle Association's prestigious Downtown Champion award for promoting the livability of the central city. Like HRG, Plymouth has been responsible for thousands of units, many in renovated older hotels and former office buildings. Many other nonprofit organizations are active in providing housing, meals, and services.

In the middle of the hip Belltown neighborhood sits a YWCA-sponsored building called Opportunity Place. It provides housing for "at-risk" women and a day shelter. Although the population it serves is at the bottom of the socioeconomic ladder, the YWCA knew its facility had to be permanent, solid, and dignified.

The seven-story structure is concrete with warm brick facing and artfully designed metal trim. Broad glass and steel canopies over the sidewalk provide protection from rainfall for residents and passersby. Surrounding the building on all sides are market-rate apartments and condominiums, none of which lost value as the result of the project's presence. To be sure, some social services do require appropriate monitoring to ensure safety of both the clientele and nearby residents, but encounters between widely varying types of people can be an enriching and humbling part of urban living.

A few blocks away is a facility called the Urban Rest Stop. It offers showers, lockers, and restroom facilities for homeless people and is supported and managed by a nonprofit with help from private sector contributions. The Metropolitan Improvement District—another offshoot of

DSA—hires formerly homeless people to clean sidewalks, monitor public spaces, and offer information to visitors. This program has made a noticeable difference in the civility of downtown streets.

Clearly, Seattle—and in particular, its business community—recognizes that to be healthy, a downtown must accommodate a wide range of people, including those who are less fortunate. Encouraging diversity means paying attention not only to different cultures, but different incomes as well.

Oakland

A few years ago, Oakland-based architect Michael Pyatok began working on a residential project a few blocks away from downtown on the edge of the city's Chinatown. But rather than leap into the typical design process, Pyatok sat down with residents and asked them what they would like to see in the new development. What emerged was a fascinating mix.

First, rather than one monolithic development occupying an entire block, the development is composed of several elements. The old Swan's Market building was renovated into retail with housing above. A new cohousing element was added that used upper-level space

Fig. 2-6. Swan's Market in Oakland, California, combines affordable and market-rate housing within a combination of renovated and new structures. It also provides needed open space for the neighborhood. Source: Pyatok and Associates, Architects.

under the trusses of the roof to create open, loft-like living spaces. A second-level gallery is shared by residents and decorated with artwork.

On the ground, a small interior courtyard was carved out of the complex for the entire public to enjoy. Folks can be seen lounging about, chatting, eating lunch, and playing with children in tow. There is a weekly farmers market on one of the adjacent streets and on those days the place feels like an exotic bazaar, with sights and smells and food and music brought in by people from dozens of different cultures.

Oakland's 10K Initiative

In 1999, Mayor Jerry Brown set a four-year goal to add 10,000 new residents to downtown Oakland by encouraging the development of 6,000 housing units on as many as 30 to 40 city blocks. This initiative launched a comprehensive planning effort by city staff, including a market study to estimate demand for rental and for-sale housing and identifying "opportunity sites"—areas comprised of at least 20,000 square feet owned by fewer than six parties and for which the value of physical improvements was less than the land value. The city concluded that demand was strong for one- and two-bedroom units within the downtown area for low-rise, moderately priced housing; luxury mid- and high-rise housing; and live/work units.

Approximately 60 sites were identified and the city projected that they could provide housing for up to 19,000 new residents. Community meetings solicited input from citizens, developers, architects, and other professionals. The city and the redevelopment authority allocated funding for downtown streetscape improvements, new sewers, and other capital improvements. Because almost no housing had been built downtown in quite a few years, information was not available to developers, lenders, or appraisers regarding land value, construction costs, or expected revenues. To start the ball rolling, Oakland's redevelopment authority initiated four market-rate housing projects, which have helped stimulate more housing on adjacent lots. Oakland also created a one-stop permit process and in 2001, the California legislature allowed streamlined environmental impact reporting for most housing projects downtown.

By January 2006, the 10K Initiative resulted in the completion of 17 projects (1,663 units). Fifteen more projects (2,144 units) are in construction and 20 additional projects (2,196 units) have been approved. Another 12 (1,922 units) are in the initial planning stages. This program will have produced almost 8,000 units in over 60 residential projects and will more than meet the original goal.

Pyatok was careful to work with architects of other nearby projects to achieve a diversity of designs. The block seems vibrant, sparkling, and even a bit eccentric, with unusual forms, colors, and textures. The various residential pieces literally reflect the cultural diversity that makes up the district.

REFERENCES

Eugenie Birch. 2005. "Who Lives Downtown Today (And Are They Any Different from Downtowners of Thirty Years Ago?)" Lincoln Institute of Land Policy, May.

Breen, Ann and Rigby, Dick, 2004. *Intown Living: A Different American Dream* Washington, D.C.: Island Press.

3

Constant Change, Many Choices

The second half of the 20th century presented us with a tragedy: Our choices in the types of housing available in this country decreased as the market began building almost exclusively detached, single-family houses. Low-interest home loans, tax-deductible mortgage interest, and the development of the Federal Interstate Highway System set in motion a series of events and changes. Financial incentives were tilted towards the massive, outward expansion of subdivisions. Types of housing that had been available and acceptable for decades, such as duplexes, row houses, and stacked flats, suddenly were shoved aside in favor of the free-standing house on its own lot. In fact, some communities even took these other forms of housing out of their codes, making them illegal to build. It took several decades to see the full effect of this transformation.

What started out as an effort to broaden the choices of Americans by opening up new places to live and work has, over time, produced the opposite effect. Many aspects of our economy, such as retailing and home building, used to be different for different regions and even cities. Now, virtually all retailing involves national brands offering the same merchandise whether the customer is in Albany, Akron, or Albuquerque. Moreover, what used to be a place-specific industry—the design and construction of houses—now either follows typical templates or is, in fact, built by large corporations whose territory is coast to coast. It is now possible to buy the same neocolonial home in Virginia, where there is at least a history of that building type, or Las Vegas, where there is none.

Streets within cities used to have distinctly localized flavor. But they began to become homogenized with the introduction of standards promulgated by federal agencies and professional engineering societies. Narrow, tree-lined lanes found in New England were deemed unsafe and unsuitable for large delivery, garbage, and fire trucks. Winding, wooded roads in the West were viewed as inefficient and difficult to maintain. In a matter of 30 years, many of our communities were radically altered, essentially to be convenient for moving vehicles.

At the same time, the civil engineering profession lost virtually all of the artfulness displayed in previous decades. Many of our most beautiful bridges, boulevards, and landscaped parkways were designed by engineers who understood the principles of composition, contrast, and context. Not anymore: Streets and roads are essentially designed according to manuals, with rigid, "no exception" numerical standards that leave little room for creativity. So far has this profession fallen away from the notion of "civil" engineering that some within it have actually prohibited trees from being planted along streets, claiming that they pose hazards to drivers. Roads and streets now look the same everywhere—wide, barren, and bereft of any character, much less charm.

The city-planning profession has not been much better. For decades, planning agencies photocopied zoning codes from other communities or national publications, rarely questioning whether the provisions made sense for their community's history, climate, topography, or economy. Some regulations, such as single-use zoning districts, large minimum lot sizes, deep setbacks, and low maximum lot coverage, virtually guaranteed a pattern of development that was low rise, low density and scattered across the landscape.

Consequently, what has happened is that Americans' choices have become narrower. Strip malls are the main way of providing goods and services. Single-family detached housing is the only "acceptable" form of living; people living in apartments are suspect or second class. Office parks and industrial parks dot the countryside, looking identical whether in the deserts of Arizona, the forests of Idaho, or the plains of Oklahoma.

Zoning-induced patterns of development, together with one-size-fits-all street standards, mean that it is necessary to do everything by automobile. There is simply not sufficient density in most communities to support public transportation—this despite the fact that many children and the elderly could benefit greatly from such systems. Instead, communities have been designed by law and by administrative rule to cater to a narrow range of ages, incomes, and lifestyle.

So much investment in infrastructure was made to produce this effect that central cities, and downtowns, in particular, suffered from corresponding and massive disinvestments. What was not accomplished by deliberate public policy was done by decisions of banks and corporations to abandon their presence in many inner city locations.

Fortunately, in the last decade many people have concluded that they prefer different sets of choices. Denser cities and their downtowns offer these choices. Even better, a characteristic of central cities is that they continually change, presenting people with new choices and dimensions and adding layers of richness, new entrepreneurial energy, and individualized goods and services.

And even more promising is that many cities—not just large ones, but even mid-sized cities and small towns—are rediscovering the virtues of encouraging change and broadening choices. They know that density is the key to both.

REDISCOVERING THE VIRTUES OF DENSITY

Thirty-five years ago, First Avenue in downtown Seattle was a red-light district. The Hollywood film *Cinderella Liberty*, in which Marsha Mason played a down-and-out hooker and James Caan a hard-drinking, roughhousing sailor, can now be viewed as a sort of urban archaeological documentary of that era. For 20 blocks the street was lined with strip joints, taverns, X-rated movie houses and bookstores, pawnshops, flophouses, and cheap cafes.

But as in all good cities, things change. Over the past three decades, virtually all of the tawdriness has disappeared, save for a couple of exotic dance parlors. One of them, the Lusty Lady (now owned by women), is across the street from the venerable Seattle Art Museum. The marquee taunts art patrons by racy come-ons with double entendres, such as "Come See Our Nudes." Rumor has it that some of the catchy taglines were composed by museum staffers.

The first wave of change came with the renovation of Pike Place Market in the early '70s. This expansive collection of fishmongers, fruit and vegetable sellers, and ethnic restaurants spurred a turnaround in the immediate neighborhood. Upscale restaurants sprung up on the adjoining blocks. Next, older historic structures, some with upper floors that had been empty for years, were converted to housing (much of it affordable) and hotels.

The aforementioned art museum built its new home along the street, and art galleries, bookstores, and coffeehouses followed soon after. Then came the specialty shops with trendy clothing, shoes, furnishings, and imported goods. Finally, new housing was built, and now virtually every block along the entire length of the street contains housing in some form.

And the street continues to change. The art museum is now tripling its size and new hotels are going up. Even more restaurants line the sidewalks—and none of them are national chains. While some businesses seem to secure a long-term presence, others come and go, giving the street a dynamic, evolving quality. It is always possible to be surprised.

Fig. 3-1. Many downtown residential neighborhoods have streets filled with small shops, services, and cafes, much like the main street of small towns. Source: LMN Architects.

And the sidewalks themselves are livelier. Street musicians play instruments on certain corners both day and night. Flower sellers display bouquets to passersby. Sidewalk cafes serve as places to meet friends during the day and become boisterous "scenes" at night. The street simply teems with energy.

Downtowns and the neighborhoods around them thrive with these changes. They are constantly being reinvented, reinfused with new people, new businesses, new "handprints." It is always fascinating to watch a new business make an effort to draw itself into the street—and, by extension, draw the street into itself. Clothing shops put sales racks on the sidewalk. Hair salons put out little sandwich board signs. Cafes arrange tables and chairs in the sun or shade.

Some businesses have rediscovered the marvelous invention of the crank-out awning, a device that dramatically alters the streetscape and reflects the seasons. Some businesses will band together to hire people to sweep the sidewalks, wash display windows, and even monitor behavior. This is the classic "main street" mentality so treasured by Americans and almost lost during the dark decades of the late 20th century.

What is also interesting to observe is the number of cities that are finally discovering how to "get it right" using the basic, time-tested principles of density and diversity, especially at the street level. For far too long, cities adopted suburban approaches that seemed to deny their value as urban places. For example, Atlanta went through decades of building skywalks, interior atriums, and fortress-like towers set on top of imposing bases. Its downtown is essentially now stultified in an antiurban attitude that sees city life as something to be feared.

Ironically, Atlanta has recently rediscovered the more classic principles of creating good places in the form of the Midtown area just to the north of its older downtown. Midtown is packed with mid- and high-rise residential towers, office buildings, restaurants, and museums. But the best part is that there are no overhead walkways or atriums. Everything faces the street and reinforces the quality of the public realm. And low and behold, lots of people are walking about.

The fascinating thing is that virtually every time we have tried to re-make cities using other models than the simple one of buildings fronting on streets with ground level uses and windows, we have failed. Pedestrian malls have not worked (outside of a handful of college towns). Buildings on podiums of parking have not worked. Skywalks have not worked. Interior atriums have not worked. Scattering big parking structures around has not worked.

David Sucher, in his book, *City Comforts*, reminds us of the handful of simple rules of thumb for good streets, good neighborhoods, and good

Fig. 3-2. In less than 10 years, Atlanta's Midtown district has been transformed into a dense, mixed use neighborhood. Source: Mark Hinshaw.

cities. And if we follow them—in contrast to all the other experiments we have tried—they almost always work.

It must have been in our collective genes—certainly in our culture—to value communal commerce, because every place that has nurtured this behavior has found itself a hotbed of urban investment with folks eager to live there, work there, or both. In fact, it is evident that many people are willing to pay a premium for housing, goods, and services for the pleasures that such places offer.

Most people prefer having choices. Why else would we surround ourselves with so many different makes of cars, brands of soup, and labels of shirts? We have begun to realize that such choices can be found in communities, just as it is in commerce. But it takes cities, especially city centers, with their attendant density, diversity, and compactness, to provide both change and choice.

TRANSFORMING SUBURBIA

What is remarkable about the current era is that density and diversity are now being seen in communities that were previously suburban in nature. Pasadena, California—perhaps the quintessential suburb—recently shed former trappings such as an internally oriented shopping mall and has evolved into a sophisticated, mid-sized city with a lively commercial core and an even more lively "old town" district. Parking lots have been replaced by multilevel garages. Dense complexes of apartments and condominiums surround the downtown, as does a collection of visual and performing arts venues.

Similar changes have been taking place throughout the country from White Plains, New York, to Vancouver, Washington. These communities are becoming cities in their own right with skylines, urban squares, transit, and dense, mixed use development. In such places, empty nesters who have lived in their community for decades are now moving to the center of town—where they can walk to a wide range of shops, services, and culture and entertainment venues.

One suburban city, in particular, has seen a transformation so dramatic as to defy even the most boosterish of its chamber of commerce-type champions. Thirty years ago, Bellevue, Washington, was a bedroom suburb of Seattle, packed with single-family detached houses and a central business district distinguished only by the number of one-story strip

Fig. 3-3. The high-rise commercial core of downtown Bellevue, Washington, is now surrounded by mid- and high-rise housing, almost all of which has been developed in the past decade. Source: Mark Hinshaw.

malls and vast seas of asphalt surrounding them. Sidewalks, where they existed, were five feet wide. Police officers would sometimes stop people who were walking because such a person might be in trouble or even suspicious.

Today, downtown Bellevue is almost completely different. While a few older, one-story buildings and parking lots still remain, this 400-acre downtown is now packed with high-rise office buildings, hotels, and dense urban housing. The city has built major new parks and a convention and performing arts center, and is renovating one of its early office buildings into a new city hall. A large regional library was built and two privately financed museums have been constructed.

In the last five years 2,000 dwellings have been developed, virtually all within mid-rise and high-rise structures. Another 2,000 are under construction or in the permitting process. This increase in urban dwellers has led to many new shops and restaurants and supported outdoor cultural events. Lincoln Square, the largest development to date, will contain a 27-story office tower, 300,000 square feet of retail space, and a 45-story tower containing a luxury hotel with condominiums above it. Despite the high prices of some of the higher units, the project is quickly selling out. A front-page story in the July 3, 2005, *Seattle Times* noted that most buyers already live in Bellevue and have simply elected to forgo their big houses to move into downtown—where "the action is."

Many of these new urban residents are not the young and hip, looking for nightlife and upscale living. They are hard-core, died-in-the-wool suburbanites, who—likely not many years ago—would have never thought of living downtown. Clearly, there is a sea change occurring with respect to consumer choices. People value density, proximity, and the presence of other people in a compact and varied setting.

SMALL TOWNS, TOO

People are rediscovering the center in some smaller communities around the country, too. Two examples are Gresham and Hillsboro, Oregon, towns located at opposite ends of the Portland metropolitan area's light-rail line. In each place, the town centers are booming with new shops and services. Around the perimeter of each downtown are growing numbers of apartments and condominiums in low-rise but dense configurations.

Snohomish, Washington (with a population of less than 9,000), is seeing housing built within close proximity to its lively, walkable downtown, which is lined with good restaurants, shops, and venues for live music. Some of this is relatively "gentle" infill development such as cottage homes and accessory dwelling units. But this new density is adding vitality and new wealth to this small, freestanding community.

Lenexa, Kansas, has so many developers eager to build a new, mixed use town center that it is having a hard time corralling all of them. The initial phase will include retail, hotel, and condominium lofts. Subsequent phases in the works include dense, low-rise residential developments, including senior housing, with neighborhood shops and services arranged around village greens. The city has made available to developers a large parcel it owns in the center for core development, including mid-rise residential, retail, civic structures, and a town square.

Clearly, the demand for "urban" amenities and atmosphere is extending to many different types and sizes of communities. It is a phenomenon not confined to coastal areas or "hip" cities and surely reflects that we are beginning a new era of appreciating dense, urban living and all the choices and dynamic changes it can offer. While many people will still continue to choose suburban or exurban lifestyles, many others will choose the centers of cities and towns. This is a long-term shift that will alter the face and feel of many communities in the coming decades.

CHANGING TOOLS AND TECHNIQUES

For hundreds of years, architects designed buildings and spaces using two elementary tools: the T-Square and the triangle. Over time each became slightly more sophisticated. The T-Square became what was called a "parallel bar," which moved up and down the drawing board on tracks or taut wires. Adjustable versions of the triangle allowed many more angles to be used. But essentially these two devices remained pretty much the same over many generations of people and many hundreds of thousands of drawings.

Meanwhile, structural engineers used simple formulas and calculations to determine how to support roofs and floors and walls. Essentially, the beam-and-column model became the norm, as structural methods evolved from load-bearing masonry to frame construction. It was simply too difficult to calculate stresses and loads on anything other than fairly simple diagrams. When the early computers appeared, more complex and sophisticated calculations became possible, but engineers were still psychologically tied to vertical and horizontal arrangements of materials.

At the same time, the plumb bob and level, used by builders since the time of the pyramids, continued to be used to erect buildings that were straight and "true."

The combination of these tools meant buildings were created by assembling rectangles—whether in plan, in elevation, or in cross section. Although there were exceptions to this, all of the parties involved in the design and construction of buildings were limited by tools that they had used without question for many, many years.

Of course, earlier cultures and civilizations were not so inclined, at least not obsessively so. Indigenous cultures produced amazing confections of building forms, some of which are popular destinations precisely because they are so dramatically different from the structures of our time. Quirky Italian hill towns, with their twisting and terraced forms, are one example. The organic, Native American pueblo dwellings in Taos, New Mexico, are another.

Today, however, computers of extreme sophistication and capability are easily available to everyone involved in design and construction. And here is the truly remarkable thing: Computers do not care if something is at a right angle. They can calculate what is required to support any kind of assembly of beams, columns, slabs, and roofs. In fact, it is often necessary to "force" a computer to draw parallel or perpendicular lines. Computers are "geometry neutral." So we are beginning to see incredible structures, dreamlike forms rising out of the ground in great

Fig. 3-4. The Central Library in Seattle defies all of the conventional notions of library design, yet is immensely successful as a civic building. Source: LMN Architects.

and sometimes odd angles, flamboyant swirls, sweeping curves, and bulbous shapes. The first generation of these new building forms can be seen in the design of art museums such as the various Guggenheims, where idiosyncratic shapes have been accepted for some time. But the big breakthrough came with Rem Koolhaas's design for the Seattle Central Library. Most libraries are clothed in staid, symmetrical, rigid forms, following unwritten rules for spatial organization, types of interior spaces, and even social use. The Seattle library breaks virtually every one of those rules and does so in a way that reflects and even celebrates the tools available to us now. It is perhaps the first major piece of architecture of the 21st century. And it is interesting to see how people react to it: Those whose idea of what libraries should look like is based on the past loathe it. Those who recognize that it reflects our time and our technologies love it.

Like architecture, city planning has been bound up by its own traditions and its own tools. While these may have been useful in the past, they are of little value now. And for cities and downtowns where diversity, density, and urbanity are valued, they are actually counterproductive.

Let's take land-use plans, for example. For many years, plans for communities were developed using maps. Sections of a city or town were colored according to anticipated or preferred uses. Red stood for commercial use. Yellow was for residential use. Gray was used for industrial areas, and so on.

For urban areas, where change occurs continually and many choices within close proximity are desired, this technique has at least three serious flaws.

First, it is two-dimensional. As we all know, cities reach into the sky with many levels of activities and human habitation. There is a development rising of the ground not far from where I live that will contain retail, residential, hotel, and office uses in multiple towers on top of a base of underground parking. How would that be colored on a two-dimensional map?

In fact, the notion of dividing communities into distinct districts or "zones" came from an attempt to address the severe and unhealthy conditions found in industrial-era cities of the late 1800s, when steel mills and slaughterhouses were located within a stone's throw of people's homes. The initial idea of pulling radically incompatible uses apart has been transmogrified over the past century to mean that it is undesirable to mix neighborhood shops with homes. Some citizens even have come to expect (and demand) that different forms of housing—even if only slightly different—be rigidly segregated.

Typically, segregated land-use plans are directly translated into zoning ordinances that also segregate uses, sometimes to an extent that desirable patterns of behavior are wiped out. For example, in the last 50 years, communities all over the country have made the corner market illegal. For most of our history, we have had a tradition of small shops and services right within neighborhoods, drawing from a local trade area. But this type of small-scale business was taken away with the rush toward exclusive, single-use land-use maps and their implementing ordinances.

If we are to regain healthy, balanced communities in which walking is reinstituted as a means of transportation, we must shed off this dysfunctional tool of two-dimensional land-use plans. Unfortunately, so ingrained is this notion that land-use plans are often cited as essential requirements of community plans in state enabling laws. Note that even the title land-use "plan" (rather than "planning") reflects a rigid idea of community organization.

This rigidity is the second fundamental flaw. Land-use plans are static; they do not reflect changes over time. If we have learned anything from the last two boom and bust recessionary periods in the economy, we must surely know that many elements of the marketplace, the products we choose, and the activities we engage in are continually changing.

Let's pick another example: the gray color used to denote industrial use on the zoning map. The selection of the color gray itself embodies the idea that industry is noxious and must be relegated to undesirable locations, along freeways or rail lines. Of course, some industries are truly incompatible with many other uses—a chemical plant might be such an example. But many economic activities no longer deserve to be painted (literally) with a gray brush.

Many years ago, in the town where I attended college, there was a factory that made graduation class rings and other ceremonial jewelry. It was a big operation, contained in a sizable one-story building. Rather than being located in an industrial park, it sat smack in the middle of an upscale neighborhood of large, single-family houses. In terms of appearance and function, the business was little different from a school. It had a pleasant brick facade. It was surrounded by well landscaped grounds and parking lots. Deliveries were made to a nicely screened loading dock. It was, in short, a good neighbor.

Today, there are thousands of businesses that could easily fit within neighborhoods. And it might just be possible for some employees to live close enough to walk to their jobs. But we are still using antiquated use zones that dictate separations.

Another reason that gray doesn't work anymore is that the form of commerce can change over time and can even embody several different types of activities within the same building. What overall use designation would you give to a business that has a retail shop along the street front, a repair shop behind it, a fabrication area behind that, a warehouse behind that, and a distribution dock to the rear for panel trucks (similar in size to the minivans found in residential areas)? Such a place might make or distribute handheld computers, medical devices, or scientific measuring equipment. It might even look like a modest, low-rise office building. So why should we force it to be only found near true industrial operations?

And uses change over time. There are several schools in my city that were saved because of their fine architecture and now contain housing. One has shops and cafes on the ground floor. Neighbors who live in the nearby detached single-family houses not only have a wonderful landmark still anchoring the neighborhood, but can walk to pick up a bottle of wine or have dinner in a nice restaurant. So what color should the former school, now residential/retail, be given on a map?

We have simply carried this idea of separate land-use districts and discrete land uses to the point of lunacy. That city planners and planning commissions often debate, disagree about, and anguish over precisely what use designation should be granted is almost Swiftian in its absurdity. Who cares whether it's a brewpub that serves food or a restaurant that serves beer?

Finally, city planners have often called for the land-use plan to "govern" local decision making when it comes to development and public investment. Planners often get themselves immersed in debates with public works professionals about whether land use or transportation should be the driver in the planning process.

As heretical as it may sound to some planners, focusing on transportation elements is much more likely to influence urban form and allow for change and choice than emphasizing land use. Of course, this means *all* forms of transportation, not just those associated with moving automobiles. Buses, streetcars, light rail, and heavy rail must be part of the picture. Bicycle facilities, trails, and adequate sidewalks are also vital. Investment in circulation and connectivity is for the long term-spanning generations. During that same time, various types of land uses can come and go. So it is important to get the transportation network right, which means not leaving it to the engineers and their manuals.

Fortunately, national engineering societies such as the Institute for Traffic Engineers and the American Society of Civil Engineers have begun to come around to more innovative ways of addressing circulation. They

Fig. 3-5. United Nations Plaza in San Francisco has recently been reenergized by a new public market that serves nearby residents and workers. Source: Mark Hinshaw.

publish reports on skinny streets, traffic calming, roundabouts, shared parking, and a host of other subjects that reflect the need to deal with urban conditions of change and choice. Unfortunately, many public works officials at the local and even state levels have not kept up with their own professional research and are mired in inflexible models and standards.

Moreover, the debate between land use and transportation ignores another important element in urban form that is equally, if not more, important: the quantity, quality, and character of public spaces. Parks, plazas, squares, greens, boulevards, and sidewalks constitute the shared, public "living rooms" for people in denser urban centers.

In recent decades, we have let many of these places fall into disrepair or become socially dysfunctional or downright unsafe. And another unfortunate tragedy is that parks departments have tended to adopt suburban open-space standards that ignore or discount the value of purely "civic" space. Most parks departments build, operate, and maintain recreational facilities. Smaller, passive urban spaces are rarely promoted. Yet it is these types of public spaces that are most appropriate and valued in dense urban settings.

Where they have been designed, built, and programmed with both thoughtfulness and verve, such spaces are immensely popular. The recently opened Jamison Square in Portland's Pearl District is filled with people of all ages. On any given warm afternoon, scores of children dressed in swimsuits play in the fountain, which surges and recedes like a surf. Young couples neck. People sprawl on the grass reading books and newspapers. Elderly people gab away over chessboards. All within a few yards of each other.

These kinds of spaces are what make cities not just livable, but great. They are investments for the long term. Together with a system of carefully thought out circulation choices, they constitute an armature that is enduring and relatively fixed. Over time, different uses and buildings can swirl about them, creating neighborhoods and districts, aging and being renewed again, giving life to the city.

In the end, fussing over land use is pretty insignificant and irrelevant. Downtowns and their close-in neighborhoods can thrive on just about any combination of uses. It all depends upon their design, their sense of neighborliness, and a recognition that they are not freestanding islands, but part of a larger community.

Change and choice, diversity and density, in multiple layers accumulated over time—that is what city centers are all about.

REFERENCE

Sucher, David. *City Comforts: How to Build an Urban Village.* Seattle: City Comforts, Inc. 2003.

4

Commerce, Culture, and Quirkiness

Over the four or five decades that followed World War II, North American cities suffered. Many families and much of the tax base shifted to fast-growing suburbs. Downtowns witnessed dramatic disinvestment. Certain inner city neighborhoods were redlined by banking institutions. And public transportation suffered as people shifted to using private automobiles.

But two elements of city life saw a particularly acute decline. The long-standing tradition of small, independent, family-owned businesses began to disappear as large corporations invaded virtually every part of our economy. And many of our "foundational" institutions—city governments, museums, theatres—were cast aside as citizens hunkered down in single-family subdivisions.

Many people now lament the loss of the local hardware store, where one could get personal service to find an obscure washer for the kitchen sink. Or the local drug store, where the pharmacist would greet family members by name. A hallmark of many neighborhoods within cities and towns was often the local cafe, where people would conduct business, meet friends, and celebrate birthdays and anniversaries.

Such "Third Places" serve an important function in society, allowing for social connections to be forged and maintained, as Ray Oldenburg has pointed out. Furthermore, Robert Putnam has documented the decline in belonging to organizations in his book, *Bowling Alone*. This combined fracturing of physical settings and social structures has created voids that are now being noticed.

In a sense we have done this to ourselves. Public policy and consumer behavior pushed people into low-density patterns of development in which small businesses, which draw largely from walk-in trade, had no chance of survival. Many people have elected to patronize the large national chains, despite their reputations for questionable labor practices and purchasing policies that flaunt their corporate power.

Similarly, public and civic institutions have been shoved to the side. City halls, libraries, and even schools were housed in the meanest, cheapest structures—almost as if we were embarrassed by them. The arts suffered as people's preferences switched to what was available on television.

But there are signs that this era is coming to an end. Many people feel culturally impoverished and have been demanding more and better artistic expression. Many cities are rediscovering that city halls, libraries, and museums serve as critical landmarks and anchors to community life, and are investing in new buildings that display a more traditional sense of stature, vitality, and dignity. We may have realized what we have lost by disregarding the "civic realm" and are now rapidly looking for ways to regain it.

BRINGING BACK SMALL BUSINESSES

In the late 1990s, downtown Springfield, Missouri, was all but dead. Department stores had abandoned the district, leaving empty, multistory shells. Forlorn-looking storefronts on the blocks surrounding the central town square were either vacant or occupied by marginal tenants barely holding on. It was possible to walk down any street and hardly see a soul.

But today, downtown Springfield is thriving; not entirely robust perhaps, but clearly on the way back up. A number of first-class restaurants have opened and are full even on weekday evenings. There are art galleries and unique clothing shops. A local coffee bar is packed day and night with clientele chatting with friends or hunkered down over laptops. A classic old theatre has been restored and offers live performances. Several nightspots offer live music.

A couple of nearby parks offer places to linger near cascading water. Outdoor concerts and plays are presented during warmer months. A new minor league baseball park, housed in a traditional stadium clad in warm brick and steel, serves as a new landmark.

The city is in the process of relocating 19th-century railroad tracks that once served mills and meatpacking houses so that a large downtown park can be created.

Developers cannot convert the older masonry buildings found throughout downtown into lofts fast enough. Some of the lofts are residences; others are filled with small businesses.

Colleen Sundlie runs a public relations business tucked into a second-story brick-lined loft on Park Central Street, a stone's throw from the town square, which has a rich and varied history stretching back to the Civil War. This gregarious young entrepreneur lives with her husband and young child in another loft right next door. When the couple throws open their big front windows overlooking the street below, sounds of music from a club on the next block waft in.

Sundlie finds the energy of living and working downtown to be inspiring. She has contracts all over the country, but chooses to live in Springfield for its small-town friendliness. Her office space is casual, with a somewhat edgy professional style. Sundlie is one of thousands of young entrepreneurs who are discovering that downtowns offer a combination of genuine history and creative energy.

Like Springfield, Coeur d'Alene, Idaho, was—for most of its history—an industrial town. Huge mills cut and processed lumber harvested from nearby forests. The downtown served the workers who lived in modest bungalows surrounding the town center. When the mills began closing—all but two are gone, and even they will not be around for long—the town temporarily lost its reason for being.

Located on a lake, and not far from mountains, the town had marketable natural amenities. In fact, in the late 1980s, a resort hotel was built on the edge of the lake a block from Sherman Avenue, the main street. But the resort complex, as attractive as it was, failed to reenergize the downtown. It was only when property owners and businesses banded together to create a new vision for the place that it began to turn around.

In the early '90s Sherman Avenue was struggling. Vacancy levels and business turnovers were high. Today, virtually every storefront is full and new housing is being built not only around the edges of downtown but within the core itself. The merchants have a coordinated marketing strategy and sponsor public art programs that give the town center an ever-changing, whimsical charm.

So successful has the turnaround been that Coeur d'Alene is attracting new, urban-scale investment. An 11-story condominium tower was built and sold out a couple of years ago. An 18-story tower is under construction, with half the units presold. Nearby, a mid-rise loft style building is about to start, and another high-rise has been proposed. Clearly, this town of 40,000 is on the verge of an astonishing transformation.

Fig. 4-1. High-rise housing is appearing in unexpected locations, such as in Coeur d'Alene in northern Idaho. Source: Mark Hinshaw.

Brad and Cynthia Hoppie own Optique, an eyewear shop on Sherman Avenue. Several years ago, the young couple moved into town after living for years in another part of the country. They were seeking a place that was intimate and sociable. Their daughter plays on the floor of the narrow shop while Brad works on orders at the back counter. The family dog lies across the threshold to the store, giving a nod to customers as they enter.

The Hoppies represent a return to the local family-owned personal services that used to be a hallmark of American commerce. No national chain with generic displays and drive-by marketing gimmicks here; you can be assured that by patronizing the store you will soon know the shopkeeper by name and he will know yours. Friends drop in for a quick chat on their way to lunch and social bonds are cemented in ways that are simply not possible with corporate franchises.

Cynthia is active in the community, helping organize her neighbors to plant display gardens. She sits on civic committees and participates in the process of local democracy.

She is articulate, opinionated, and yet warmly receptive to other people's ideas and perspectives.

The Seattle metropolitan area is extremely fortunate to have a developer who does not fit the typical mold. Ron Sher is an anomaly; some of his peers might even call him a bit wacko. Rather than build up an empire of brand-spanking-new shopping centers or office buildings, he

Fig. 4-2. Crossroads in Seattle, once a failed mall, is now the center of community life for the diverse ethnic neighborhoods surrounding it. Source: Mark Hinshaw.

buys places of commerce that seem to be at the end of their lives. With his homespun acumen, he almost magically transforms them into local icons—places that neighbors see as the psychic, if not physical, center of their communities.

Twenty years ago he bought an all-but-dead shopping center in the eastern suburbs of Seattle. In a few years the place was teeming with new life. Playing off the growing ethnic attributes of the surrounding district, he added a slew of small specialty food stands. He discarded portions of the vast parking lot and built small shops facing outward. He filled the buildings with new tenants and hired a vivacious woman to program the place with community events, musical performances, festivals, and art shows. He painted a huge chessboard on the floor of the former mall and invited people to hang out and play the game with person-sized chess pieces. One of the new tenants was Third Place Books—a used bookstore he named in honor of Ray Oldenburg's work.

So successful was Third Place Books that Sher opened a second store in another failed mall north of Seattle. In this one he added food sellers around the edges and a stage for cooking classes and performances off to one side. He threw in dozens of chairs and several overstuffed sofas. And he invited folks in to simply hang out. Since the day it opened, the store has been packed from 8 a.m. to midnight.

More recently, he purchased the independent Elliott Bay Bookstore in downtown Seattle, which was days away from going under due to competition of national chains. He kept the name but infused it with a new energy and made sure the staff continued to provide the same informed and personable service the store had been known for.

Sher himself is fairly modest in both attitude and accoutrements. He lives in an unassuming home where he occasionally holds soirees for visiting authors. Oldenburg is a repeat guest. Sher has managed to combine his entrepreneurial skills with his passion for literature. He sees his developments not just as profit centers, but as community centers.

He seeks little credit but is heaped with praise. Communities beg for him to set up shop in their towns.

CULTIVATING CULTURE

Like many other North American cities, Kansas City saw successive booms of high-rise office development in its downtown during the late 20th century. The result is a clutch of generic, glass-and-steel towers flanked by lifeless plazas. Small shops were replaced by block-long facades, many occupied by banks. One can walk along some sidewalks in midday and hardly see another person.

Fig. 4-3. Local artists and small businesses have infused Wyandotte Street in Kansas City with a quirkiness that makes it unique. Source: LMN Architects.

A couple of dozen blocks to the southwest of downtown, there is a spark of promise. On Wyandotte Street, a group of artists has occupied a building and filled it with one-of-a-kind shops. Nearby, art galleries and studios are springing up. Folks decorated with tattoos lounge about at the local coffeehouse. In a nearby alley, a gardener tends to a tiny pea-patch.

Old warehouse buildings are being renovated into apartments. New buildings are being erected on former parking lots. Banners proclaim "New Lofts for Lease." Clearly, this is an emerging new neighborhood fueled by the edgy, urban-pioneering efforts of a handful of local artists. In recent decades, artists have often been the bellwether of reinvestment in center cities. They often require more space and a somewhat industrial atmosphere in which to engage in welding, create large-scale constructions, and move pallets of materials. They are willing to live in surroundings that are noisier and more rough-edged than other neighborhoods.

Similar versions of this phenomenon have occurred in other cities. Although its citywide population has declined, St. Louis has seen the transformation of former warehouses near the center into a whole new neighborhood called the Washington Avenue Loft District. Old brick structures have been adapted into housing; the neighborhood's centerpiece is the City Museum, which interprets the community's industrial heritage. Art galleries, theaters, restaurants, and nightclubs are part of the lively mix, which appeals to both empty nesters and young singles and couples. Jim Cloar of the St. Louis Downtown Partnership said in an interview with Lucy Ferriss of the *New York Times*, "People are moving back from exurbia. Our motto is 'Live it up downtown.'"

In a March 26, 2006, article in the *New York Times* entitled "In Denver, Home is Where the Art Is," writer Mindy Sink noted the tremendous appeal that cultural institutions have with respect to attracting investments in dense housing. Sink highlighted the new urban developments being built within close proximity to both the new Denver Art Museum and the new Museum of Contemporary Art. It seems that many arts patrons are electing to live near their cultural interests.

In some cities nonprofit organizations have been created to ensure that artists living downtown do not get gentrified out. Artspace, headquartered in Minneapolis, was formed in 1979 precisely to assist artists in finding affordable locations within center cities. After initially serving as an advocacy group, Artspace realized that it would need to take on a development role to ensure that its mission was realized. In the last 15 years, more than a dozen older structures in the Minneapolis-St. Paul area have been renovated for occupancy by artists and arts organizations.

An early success was the Northern Warehouse Artists Cooperative in St. Paul's Lowertown Historic District. The large, chunky brick building now provides 52 live-work spaces. Another Artspace project, the Tilsner, is next door. The presence of a thriving group of artists has clearly reinvigorated the formerly derelict Lowertown, a district that is now home to more than 200 residents. Lowertown is now considered one of that city's most lively and sought-after locations to live. But the best part of this turnaround is that, because of the efforts of Artspace, market forces will not displace the artists and the energy they bring.

In Minneapolis, Artspace has been responsible for the Traffic Zone Center for the Arts, which has 24 spacious studios. The Hennepin Center for the Arts, housed within a former Masonic Temple, is one piece of an ensemble of structures that will form the Minnesota Schubert Performing Arts and Education Center. Another current project is Grain Belt Studios, which occupies part of an old brewery. As a metropolitan area, the Twin Cities have emphasized the arts for many decades. Now it can be sure that artists will continue to contribute to the daily life of the region.

Artspace has been exporting its expertise to other cities. In recent years, it has taken on similar renovation projects in Buffalo, Houston, Miami, Reno, Pittsburgh, and Seattle. Cities all over the country are

Fig. 4-4. Artspace has gained a national reputation for converting older industrial buildings into live-work space for artists, such as this one in Minneapolis. Source: Artspace Projects.

realizing how important it is to nurture their homegrown culture.

For many years, downtown Tacoma, Washington, was the laughing-stock of the Puget Sound metropolitan area. Dirty and smelly, it reeked from the wood pulp mills that dotted the waterfront. Downtown had been decimated. Most retailers had departed for outlying malls. Many older structures were empty, despite their wonderful Victorian-era character.

After several failed attempts at using urban renewal—building a pedestrian mall, then ripping it out; building several incredibly ugly parking garages, then regretting it—the city tried another tack. About 15 years ago, it started on a course of building the finest cultural venues it possibly could. The start was relatively modest, though heroic for a city that was essentially on the skids.

The city first took on the restoration and refitting of the historic Pantages Theatre, an ornate former movie palace that stood at one end of the downtown. Since its reopening, the theater has hosted hundreds of traveling Broadway shows, dance, musicals, and other events. A new theater for the resident Tacoma Actors Guild was built next door.

Several years later the Rialto, another old movie house a block away, was restored and opened for films and locally produced events. Tacoma now had a thriving performing arts district.

Bolstered by this success, the city convinced the federal government to locate its court facility in the old Union Station. A combination of restoration and new construction, the domed former station is not only the lobby for the courthouse, but it has been the setting for numerous cultural and community events. Beneath the dome hang several enormous glass sculptures made by internationally known glass artist Dale Chihuly, who was born in Tacoma and still maintains a presence there.

Next door, Tacoma worked with Washington state to build a new state history museum. The former building was outside of downtown, hardly noticed by anyone. The new structure, designed by Charles Moore, includes bold arches that play off the geometry of the train station-turned-courthouse. Thousands of school children now have access to an expansive and well-presented collection that interprets their regional heritage.

Next, the city worked with the University of Washington to renovate a handful of old warehouse buildings into space for a downtown branch campus. More than half a dozen older buildings have been given new life—including an old power plant that is the campus library—and several new structures have been built that fit in with the historic character. A master plan calls for 16 city blocks to be gradually converted to academic use and housing, all arranged around a sweeping, central green space that terraces down the hillside. The initial phases of this space are open to the public. All around the urban campus, private developers have bought up other old warehouses and converted them to housing.

Subsequently, a massive community fund-raising effort led to plans to attract a world-class architect to design a new home for the Tacoma Art Museum. For years the museum had occupied an old bank building in space that was cramped and difficult to service. The $23 million, gleaming angular metal museum structure now anchors the center of downtown.

Finally, Tacoma collaborated with Dale Chihuly to construct a huge new museum devoted to glass art. This whimsical building, roughly modeled after old cone-shaped industrial structures, serves as a new landmark for the downtown. With so many cultural venues, sidewalks that were not long ago devoid of people are now bustling with activity.

And best of all, now that there is a critical mass of energy and investment in the downtown, people are queuing up to build housing there—something that has not been seen in decades. Since 2001, almost 1,500 units have been built in more than a dozen buildings. From this spectacular example, it is evident that nurturing arts and culture can be a powerful economic development tool.

URBAN QUIRKINESS

Frank's Diner sits on the edge of downtown Spokane, Washington. It occupies an ornate railroad car that once served as the tail end of a whistle-stopping presidential train. Velvet booths flank an aisle at the far end, while a long counter with stools is up front. Patrons at the counter are entertained by short order cooks flipping pancakes, scrambling eggs, and shouting out "order up!"

The waitstaff is chatty and affable. Once I unwittingly dropped my keys as I was leaving. One of the staff found them and went to the trouble of tracking me down by calling the airport. Since I was minutes from boarding my flight, she offered to mail them to my home.

Frank's is an anomaly in contemporary American commerce. We have unfortunately become used to national brands with their standard fare, minimal service, and workers who seem to barely tolerate being at their workstations. The folks who work at Frank's clearly enjoy what they do and value their customers. People who eat there often have broad smiles as they chat with staff. Eating at Frank's can make one's day brighter and richer. It is a truly unique place ... somewhat odd and definitely quirky.

A few blocks away from Frank's is an emerging downtown neighborhood. In what used to be flophouses, beat-up buildings, and tired storefronts is now an eccentric collection of renovated apartments, condominiums, lofts, and one-of-kind shops. The Rocket Bakery anchors one corner; its large, roll-up doors allow tables and chairs to spill out onto the sidewalk. The Rocket seems to always have at least one person who is a "character" on the premises.

Ron Wells is the person largely responsible for turning this formerly ragtag part of Spokane around. One by one, he has acquired older buildings, renovated them, and filled them with new uses. One of the most challenging and most unusual structures was a massive steam plant with immense rooms filled with boilers and pipes and topped by a pair of skyscraper-high smokestacks.

Today the building is filled with a lively bar and restaurant. Patrons dine sitting on former catwalks and even inside an old, scrubbed-out boiler. Wells kept as much of the old interior as he could and the space is not unlike being inside an Escher drawing; platforms and staircases seem to jut out at every turn.

Wells does not see his properties as some kind of urban theme park with cute signs and boutiques. The district is still very gritty and in some areas even rough. It is filled with odd bits and layers of urban history. The neighborhood continues to be a stewpot of both the seamy and the sublime. Wells built a grouping of new row houses—including one for him and his wife—right in the middle of it all. Built around the guts of an old car dealership, the sophisticated group of homes looks like it could be one of London's delightful mews. The appeal of this emerging urban neighborhood comes in part from the contrasts found within it. It is at once both comely and quirky.

Powell's Books in Portland, Oregon, is the kind of bookstore that national chains like Barnes & Noble have tried to copy. It is an immense, cavernous place with multiple levels and all sorts of nooks and crannies. Books line shelves too high, in some cases, to reach. People go to Powell's to hang out for hours, browsing and reading and chatting with fellow book lovers.

In one corner of the store a funky cafe offers coffee and handmade meals and treats. People lounge about and schmooze, working on laptops and flipping through newspapers. The service is personable and knowledgeable.

But the best part of Powell's is outside, around the store. It is the centerpiece of a district that is alive with commerce and activity day and

Fig. 4-5. The huge, labyrinthine Powell's Books in Portland is an oasis of sociability and literature surrounded by new urban housing. Source: Mark Hinshaw.

night. Small restaurants and cafes line the sidewalks. Secondhand clothing shops dot the area. Music venues open in the early evening and stay open until the early morning. Quaint small hotels occupy several older buildings. Art galleries abound. Swirling around Powell's are all manner of urban delights.

Now, it is probably unfair to attribute all of this solely to the presence of Powell's. But it certainly helped. People love choices in cities, and like choices that are offbeat and unique. Powell's demonstrates the powerful impact of businesses that cater not merely to the bottom line but to our desires for enrichment. It's an attitude toward cities and city life that can't be grown in a corporate boardroom with obsessions with branding and market share. Powell's sees itself as a part of a community—one that fosters individuality and intellectual expression in many forms.

REFERENCES

Putnam, Robert. 2000. *Bowling Alone: The Collapse and Revival of the American Community*. New York: Simon and Schuster.

Ferriss, Lucy. 2005. "In St. Louis, Old Warehouses, New Promise." The *New York Times*, October 2.

Sink, Mindy. 2006. "In Denver, Home Is Where the Art Is." The *New York Times*, March 26.

5

Streets as Public Living Rooms

At some point during the second half of the 20th century, civil engineering in America lost its way. The profession has had a long, rich history of people who were not only technically proficient but artful as well. Engineers such as John Augustus Roebling created magnificent structures that have become revered city landmarks. Bridges, boulevards, monuments, towers, abutments, and all manner of industrial structures were rendered in forms both bold and poetic.

The "civil" in the term signified a responsibility to serve a larger purpose, to create public works that were at once functional and beautiful so the public investments would be celebrated in an expressive and graceful manner. One need only traverse the beautiful drawbridges across the Chicago River or stand alongside a dam to realize the power that artfully expressed structural forces can display. The tradition goes back to Leonardo da Vinci and is expressed to this very day by Spanish engineer and architect Santiago Calatrava.

But in the United States, civil engineering has been responsible for the design of some of the most austere and mean-spirited parts of our infrastructure. We have bridges that resemble little more than freeway overpasses. Riverbanks in many communities have been turned into channels with smooth concrete embankments. Artful and expressive design gave way to design by numbers, with manuals dictating the most severe and basic applications of materials and structure.

Civil engineering spawned a whole subprofession of traffic engineering—a field dedicated solely to accommodating motorized vehicles, with no other values besides the movement and storage of automobiles and trucks. One of the worst aspects of this evolution has been the institution of the notion of Level of Service. This is a method of grading the flow of vehicles along a corridor, much like water flowing in a pipe. A few seconds of slowed traffic movement can reduce the LOS of a street from C to D. The A through F grading system is so simplistic that it is seductive; it resembles an elementary school report card. Unfortunately, hundreds of cities and towns have adopted it to influence how public dollars are spent.

The result has been the gradual weighting of virtually all investments associated with streets to be devoted to the alignment, width, and paving of the roadbed. Almost no attention has been given to people walking or using transit or bicycles. In many communities not being in a car is not merely unappealing, it is downright dangerous, because the only place to walk is on tiny strips of concrete situated within a few feet of fast-moving vehicles.

From time to time, this extreme obsession with accommodating vehicles has been met with equally extreme ideas, some of which were misguided, such as pedestrian malls, sky bridges, and underground walkways. These notions essentially capitulated to the idea that streets are principally or even *only* for vehicles; pedestrians must have their own separate spaces.

Fortunately, in the last decade or so we have discovered the poverty of viewing streets in such a way. All sorts of new forms are being built or accomplished through retrofitting. Other professions such as landscape architects and urban designers have gained influence over the design of streets. The thrust of these efforts is to once again make our public infrastructure not only meet desired functional requirements but to do so in a manner that is gracious and artful.

SOCIABLE SIDEWALKS

One of the most significant contributions of the new urbanist movement has been to reinstill the importance of the street as a basic element of community building. Moreover, it has fostered notions—many of them simply rediscoveries—of the importance of these corridors as social networks, not merely traffic conduits. Street cross sections promoted by the new urbanists always include narrowed lane widths, on-street parking, and generous sidewalks. They have even pointed to the importance of details such as maintaining a tight turning radius, also known as the curb return, at intersections. Frequently, these directions run counter to those maintained for decades by public works departments and fire marshals who see their mission as expediting the movement and speed of large vehicles.

Nonetheless, the whole idea of streets as social space is gaining momentum. In fact, this notion is central to the ability of cities to accommodate

Fig. 5-1. A host of elements, including active, outward-facing uses and design features, ensures that urban sidewalks are animated. Source: LMN Architects.

higher densities within livable neighborhoods. We simply cannot apply "ideal" standards suitable for outlying suburban places to central cities and urban neighborhoods. These places speak to the needs of people on foot, not the unimpeded circulation of cars and trucks. In fact, using the LOS scale of A to F, many wonderful streets found in urban areas now likely fall into the D and F range, as they constrict the smooth flow of traffic in favor of pedestrians.

A quintessential example of this is Pike Place, a narrow street within the Pike Place Market in Seattle. With angled parking stalls on one side, it is barely wide enough to allow for two cars to move side by side. In fact, most vehicles move single file, their speed not more than that of a person walking. People feel free to use the street, walking in between cars and trucks, as the vehicles have been "tamed" to fit with pedestrians. Even so, deliveries get made. Garbage gets picked up. And no one is dying because emergency vehicles cannot get through. The street is amazingly inclusive, even democratic. Everyone has roughly equal access. And the energy and vitality is positively palpable.

But of course, Pike Place is an exception to the general condition in which pedestrian movement occurs on sidewalks, separated from the

Fig. 5-2. Vehicles move so slowly along Pike Place in Seattle that people feel comfortable walking within the street. Source: Mark Hinshaw.

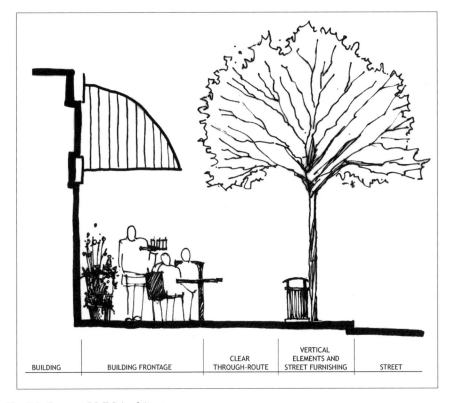

Fig. 5-3. Source: LMN Architects.

roadway. Even so, the envelope of space associated with the sidewalk has amazing possibilities to serve as places for people to spend time. In fact, urban sidewalks can serve as the predominant form of public space in denser neighborhoods, so long as certain relationships are present.

These relationships can be explained by picturing the street as a three-dimensional linear room with the sidewalk as the "floor."

The Clear Through-Route

First, there is the need for a clearly visible, easily navigable, continuous through-route. The absolute minimum width of this corridor must be 42 inches in order to meet requirements of the Americans with Disabilities Act. However, this width only accounts for a single person, in a wheelchair, traversing the route. This width is not adequate for the more common situation of two people either passing or walking side by side. To accommodate two people, at least five feet is necessary. This dimension is the result of two feet of width for each body and a little extra for a personal space bubble. (This is the case in North America;

Fig. 5-4. Maintaining a sidewalk passageway free of obstructions is important for all people, but especially for those who are visually impaired. Source: Mark Hinshaw.

other cultures have less of a need for space and will walk closer together.)

But another condition that is often found in denser places is the prevalence of three people abreast—two side by side and one passing. This increasingly common condition generates a need for at least seven feet of width. Therefore, a seven-foot-wide, clear walking path is often recommended on major streets—particularly those with retail—where more people on foot are expected. In some places with high pedestrian movement this dimension is insufficient; 10 feet is more comfortable in that it allows two people together to pass two others.

Fortunately people are fluid in their movements and even do a little dance, subconsciously determining the speed and direction of oncoming walkers and scanning for obstacles and alternate routes. Walkers will slow their gait or slightly turn the body to allow someone to pass. It is quite a spectacular bit of spontaneous, collective choreography. Rarely do people bump into or even touch one another.

The Street Tree/Vertical Elements Zone

This is the portion of the linear outdoor room that is located immediately behind the curb. At a minimum, it contains street trees. Trees need enough room to allow water and air to reach the roots. This translates into four to five feet of width and 20 to 25 square feet in area for each tree. Many cities have standards that call for trees and other objects to be set back from the curb by several feet. And it's a good idea to allow space for car doors to open and to allow people to disembark from buses and other vehicles.

The combination of these factors results in a desirable width in the range of four to six feet. Although some urban boulevards and major shopping streets may give this zone greater width, it is sufficient for most urban neighborhoods. It allows other permanent, fixed vertical elements such as streetlights, directional signs, and parking meters or pay stations to be organized into an alignment. This is also the place for many movable or temporary elements such as sandwich board signs and waste receptacles.

To create a greener effect, this zone can also be enhanced with hedges and seasonal plantings. Planting beds can be surrounded by low fencing for a more elegant touch. Decorative paving such as cobblestones and bricks can also be placed in this zone.

When Mountain View, California, reconstructed its main shopping street, it created a fascinating variation on this zone. Certain aspects of the zone were extended into the curbside parking stalls. For example, some trees were placed on "fingers" that separate pairs of stalls. The

Fig. 5-5. The design of this very active main street in Mountain View, California, includes cafe seating in areas normally used for parallel parking. Source: Mark Hinshaw.

paving pattern of the sidewalk was carried across the width of the parking stalls, and the parking stalls were raised slightly above the adjacent roadbed, causing cars to slightly mount the parking strip. The effect extends the character of the sidewalk and the tree zone further into the street. Indeed, so effective has this been that some restaurants have placed outside seating within some of the parking areas and surrounded them with planters. People seem to be comfortable having a meal within a few feet of passing cars.

Seattle has declared a number of downtown streets as "Green Streets." Within this street tree zone there is considerably more vegetation, often within sidewalk bulbs that extend into the street intersection area. One green street includes an artful placement of low stone walls within the planting bed. In a project called Growing Vine Street, the sloping street incorporates a series of terraced planters to catch and filter runoff. Artist Buster Simpson designed a whimsical blue tank to sit in one portion. An overhead pipe deflects rainfall that lands on the roof of an adjacent building and sends it into the tank for slow release into the storm system.

The Building Frontage Zone

The nature of this zone depends on the adjacent use. Sometimes the street right-of-way can be too narrow to allow for this zone to be present at all.

On streets containing predominantly residential use, this zone can contain shallow planting pockets, stoops, steps, and other features that create the effect of a small "front yard." Newbury Street in Boston has numerous long staircases in this zone, with sidewalk cafes, retail displays, or planting areas in between.

Vancouver requires new residential towers to be set back from the sidewalk to allow for planting and encourages low-rise town houses that can reinforce the vitality along the street. In Portland's Pearl District, an old railroad warehouse was adapted into housing; the former docks are now porches that are lushly planted and filled with outdoor patio furniture.

On streets where retail predominates, this is an important zone that allows shops and restaurants to spill out onto the street. This is where cafes and coffee bars can place tables and chairs. Merchants can put out displays of clothing, books, and flowers. Building lobbies can be flanked by planters and seating.

While the width of this zone can vary greatly depending on the right-of-way and the extent to which some structures are set back, it

Green Streets in Three Cities

Seattle (Departments of Planning and Development and Transportation)

Seattle's Green Streets program was enacted as a land-use code initiative, designating certain urban corridors as Green Streets to improve the pedestrian environment. Green Streets are designated through City Council action. Any future improvements to the Green Streets must follow the Green Street guidelines adopted in 1993. Incentives are provided in the form of FAR bonuses.

The success of Green Streets in Seattle has produced a wave of voluntary green streets, where owners and developers are looking for ways to introduce green design elements into their frontages, especially for streets with high pedestrian activity and low traffic volume.

Portland (Bureau of Environmental Services)

Metro, the regional government for the Portland area, has published three handbooks that provide practical information for designing green streets through its Transportation Planning Department. Portland's Sustainable Stormwater Program maintains a list of people and neighborhoods that have expressed interest in providing a green street. Sites are chosen based on neighborhood support, a unique opportunity to test for specific types of conditions, and an area that doesn't conflict with underground utilities.

Neighborhoods initially express interest in the creation of green streets in their locale. The city takes care of the plants for the first two years after installation. After two years, little maintenance is needed. City crews weed and replace dead plants, or neighborhood volunteers can help maintain them.

Vancouver, B.C. (Engineering Services)

Vancouver's Green Streets Program began in 1994 as a pilot project and its success inspired other neighborhoods to get involved. Traffic circles and corner bulges are constructed by the city, and a sign is placed on the garden area to indicate whether it is available for sponsorship. The city provides plants, free compost in spring and fall, and a newsletter for volunteers. The city maintains an inventory of all volunteers and makes sure that participation will continue each year.

Volunteers agree to work with the city and their communities to help the gardens grow throughout the year. For traffic circles that are not yet designed, opportunity is available to work with the city to create a planting plan. Each year, Green Streets gardeners are invited to the Green Streets Garden Party to meet other volunteers, share photos of the gardens, and meet city and corporate sponsors.

can be as small as several feet to as much as 15 feet. Some of the area might be within the right-of-way, while other portions might be on private property.

When done well, this zone can add a rich, diverse mixture of activity to the street. Furthermore, when building owners and shopkeepers take "ownership" over the front sidewalk, they watch over it and maintain it. In many cities, it is not uncommon to see merchants sweeping the sidewalks and placing decorative elements out in the early morning as they open. One cafe owner in my neighborhood positions himself at the doorway so that he can greet customers, keep an eye on tables, and watch over the sidewalk.

These zones and what they contain can be combined in hundreds of different ways. If they reflect the activities and tastes of adjacent residents, owners, and merchants, streets can truly sing with ever-changing delights. This is the type of street that keen observers from Jane Jacobs to Holly Whyte have praised.

MAIN STREETS

Ask Americans where they would prefer to live—big city, suburb, small town, or countryside—and they will likely say a small town. Now in some cases, this might be an example of "cognitive dissonance," in which someone is referring to the bedroom suburb they live in as a small town. Or wistful thinking about owning a big, fully restored Victorian house surrounded by an immaculate lawn and gardens. Or maybe it's simply self-delusion.

Whatever the reason, Americans revere and idealize small-town living. In a sense it is buried deep within our cultural and political roots, along with Jeffersonian democracy and colonial towns with meeting halls and village greens. We all seem to carry picture-postcard versions of a small town in our heads: tree-lined streets, genteel parks, quaint church steeples, stately courthouses, the corner grocer, and the neighborhood druggist.

The fact is, this idyllic type of community has been fast disappearing, replaced by national chains, strip malls, branding, and marketing aimed at people arriving by automobile. The small town thrived in the era when there were large families and people walked to the store, to school, and to church. We have tended to forget that many small towns were actually concentrations of fairly dense living, with lots of people who needed goods, services, and entertainment within close proximity.

Over several decades, we have seen small towns turned into suburbs, their former downtowns abandoned in favor of outlying malls

Fig. 5-6. Many close-in urban neighborhoods now have their own main streets, much like those in classic American small towns. Source: Mark Hinshaw.

and freestanding box stores. What many people now realize they are really missing is the "sense of center"—functionally, socially, and psychologically—that a main street provides to a community. The notion of a street containing a multitude of small, locally owned shops, pleasant cafes and restaurants, a movie theatre or two, and a town hall remains a strong desire despite the fracturing and fragmentation we have experienced in most communities.

It is somewhat ironic, then, that the idea of a small town main street is being revived, but within the context of a larger city. In many cities, residents refer to themselves as living in a specific area, as often as not a neighborhood that probably has a population close to the size of a small town. Many of these places contain a main street, with shops and services not unlike those in the idealized small town.

In a sense, we are seeing hundreds of small towns emerge within cities, with localized main streets that are supported by considerable concentrations of people (aka density) surrounding them. And it does take many people living close by (aka density) to support a market, a pharmacy, a movie theatre, or a library.

Main streets are important to us because they reaffirm social bonds through the simple, human act of walking about. We get to know the bank manager, the dry cleaner, and the dress shop owner on a first name basis. We develop a sense that everyone is looking after the welfare of the community as a whole. We are not alone; we have a network of people to call upon on a daily basis. This is not only comfortable, it is fulfilling. We have a chance to reaffirm humanity when we can chat with the coffee counter person, the baker, and the cafe owner. This satisfies a basic, fundamental human need for social connectedness.

An increasing number of streets in American cities are being used for markets that allow buyers to come in direct contact with fabricators. Consumers like them because they eliminate the middleman and offer lower prices in a relaxed, informal setting. Communities like them because they add richness and variety. This can be seen in the amazing array of unique products offered in the market held on a temporarily closed street in Oakland, California's Old Town, where dozens of ethnic merchants display their goods several times each week. There is a noticeable buzz as merchants and buyers circulate and converse.

On my street, local shopkeepers will trust me to bring them money later if I've forgotten my wallet. The two brothers who run my favorite restaurant chat with me as I walk in the door. The cooks in the cafe on the corner wave as I pass by the kitchen window. The druggist knows my name and dispenses useful advice. The affable woman who runs the tailoring business will replace an errant button without charge. And people in the neighborhood will often linger on the sidewalk and talk about the events of the day.

Yet I do not live in a small town, at least not literally. I live on a street in a dense urban neighborhood in the center of a major city. And this street has its counterparts in many emerging urban neighborhoods from coast to coast. Older big cities, of course, always had such places; New York, Boston, Philadelphia, and Chicago abound with them. But main streets are popping up in many cities that did not have this tradition.

In some ways, it's a product of simple math: More people living in a location equals more demand for goods and services. But it's more than that, or we would be seeing only national brands responding. It takes merchants and property owners wanting to be part of a community—making a profit, certainly, but also making connections with real people.

It is encouraging to see such a deeply rooted American preference be rediscovered amidst high rises. We love the main street, we want it nearby, and we want it to be a good place to spend time and meet friends and neighbors. And the best part is that people can, once again, *walk* to the market, the movie house, or the library.

In a very real sense, main streets offer a remedy to the congestion and impaired mobility caused by 50 years of outward sprawl. As people retire, or look for shopping that lets them be less dependent on the automobile, or seek out a lifestyle that allows giving up a car altogether, neighborhoods within close proximity to main streets will be in hot demand. Many cities are already seeing a sharp increase in the number and density of housing units being built near main streets.

It is as if many people are already seeing the future and voting with their feet. Clearly we are seeing the beginning of an era in which people value other aspects of life than simply an opportunity to drive anywhere at any time.

THE POWER OF TREES

One of my first full-time jobs was working for a landscape architecture firm in New York City that had a contract to plan and supervise the planting of street trees throughout the five boroughs. Over the course of a couple of years, I saw to the installation of more than 4,000 trees. This was an amazing experience that gave me an appreciation for the transformative effect of trees in urban places.

Whether the neighborhood was wealthy or low income, whether it was predominantly white or deeply ethnic, residents were keenly interested in seeing trees planted. People would come up to me and chat or stop and kibitz as the contractor would cut into the sidewalk pavement and drop in the tree. I was presented with gifts, invited in to have tea, given cookies and pastries—all because people desired to have growing things in their midst. It was especially touching because the city did not simply give these trees away; each neighborhood had to pay half of the cost, no small expense for some poorer places.

Now, decades later, these trees have grown large and mature. The streets feel lush where they were formerly barren. There is a visible sign of seasons changing. Birds and squirrels have found habitat. And in many cases, residents have planted minigardens in the small pits surrounding the trees. It is a powerful, primal, life-affirming activity to live with and nurture growing things. Tony Hiss, in his book *The Experience of Place*, eloquently describes the basic human need to see living things. He writes about places where people benefit from being close to what he calls "working landscapes." He passionately calls for preserving farms and other natural systems within and near cities.

Street trees play a deceptively simple role within a city. That is perhaps why they are so easily overlooked as an element that needs to be

Fig. 5-7. With all the new high-rise development in San Diego, street trees of a major scale are very important to the quality and livability of the public realm. Source: Mark Hinshaw.

cared for. Fortunately, many cities are adding urban foresters and tree biologists to their staffs so they can catalog and maintain the collection of trees along public streets.

This is increasingly necessary because, like any forest, an urban forest needs to be managed. Trees die; they get hit by vehicles; they are affected by disease and drought. There have been numerous efforts in the last 100 years to plant trees along streets. Some of those efforts were well intentioned but done without considering the peculiar needs of trees in hard-edged, urban settings. Often, citizen committees selected trees that were more appropriate for large lawns. Subsequently, roots invaded sewer lines or heaved up sidewalks. Merchants complained that their signs were being blocked or that copious amounts of leaves dropped in the fall.

The science of planting and caring for street trees has progressed considerably in the last decade or so. Some cities have approved lists of trees that are suitable for sidewalks. Others have specifications for planting and watering, sometimes requiring irrigation to ensure proper growth. Public works departments often insist upon setbacks from curb lines and intersections.

The Value of Trees in Urban Settings

MONETARY VALUE

• One mature tree can have an appraised value of between $1,000 and $10,000. (Council of Tree and Landscape Appraisers, www.almanacnews.com)

• Trees can boost the market value of a home by 6 or 7 percent. (Dr. Lowell Ponte, www.arborday.org)

• Landscaping, especially with trees, can increase property values as much as 20 percent. (Management Information Services/ICMA, www.arborday.org)

• Nationwide, trees add an average of $5,000 in value to a residential lot. (U.S. Forest Service, www.urbanforest.org.)

• The annual benefits outweigh the costs by about $54 each year for every single tree. (Tree Foundation of Kern, www.urbanforest.org.)

• Trees stimulate economic development, attracting new business and tourism. Commercial retail areas are more attractive to shoppers, apartments rent more quickly, tenants stay longer, and space in a wooded setting is more valuable to sell or rent. (The National Arbor Day Foundation, www.arborday.org)

ENVIRONMENTAL VALUE

• The net cooling effect of a young, healthy tree is equivalent to 10 room-size air conditioners operating 20 hours a day. (U.S. Department of Agriculture, www.arborday.org)

• Trees properly placed around buildings can reduce air conditioning needs by 30 percent and heating needs by 20–50 percent. (U.S. Department of Agriculture Forest Service, www.arborday.org)

• A cypress buffer two feet thick between a yard and a busy street can reduce street noise by five decibels. (Associated Landscape Contractors of America, www.igin.com)

• Properly positioned plant materials can lower heating and cooling costs by as much as 20 percent. (Associated Landscape Contractors of America, www.igin.com)

• Three strategically planted trees can provide shade that will lower cooling costs by 10 to 50 percent. (Tree Foundation of Kern, www.urbanforest.org)

• A "well-treed" neighborhood is 5–10 degrees cooler than a new development. (Tree Foundation of Kern, www.urbanforest.org)

• A single urban tree with a 50-year life span yields about $273 in environmental and economic benefits each year: air conditioning, $73 savings; stemming erosion and stormwater runoff, $75; providing wildlife shelter, $75; controlling air pollution, $50. Compounding $273 for 50 years at 5 percent yields $57,151 in benefits per urban tree. (Tree Foundation of Kern, www.urbanforest.org)

But where they are present, street trees perform an amazing array of functions. Research has shown that they create a microclimate, lowering temperatures in summer months. They provide needed oxygen to offset carbon monoxide from vehicles. They provide living quarters and food for a wide variety of birds and animals. They shade the sidewalks in summer but let the sun reach the pavement in winter.

Trees also help create urban rooms that are graceful and welcoming. Large trees lining the street help visually contain the roadway, reducing the perceived distance between curbs. Traffic tends to travel somewhat slower when trees are present, making walking safer and more comfortable. Trees also create smaller "rooms" along the sidewalk, presenting a line of demarcation that is echoed by storefronts. The resulting space is more intimate and sociable and contains a balance of both living and inanimate elements.

It is evident from mere observation that residential areas lined with street trees enjoy greater desirability, both in terms of property values and market demand. Similarly, commercial areas with street trees are more attractive to customers, visually lively, and economically vibrant. Recently, Kathleen Wolf completed extensive research on many urban streets and found solid evidence that retail streets planted with trees produce more income for merchants because people spend more time there. When planted with trees, otherwise austere arterial streets can be transformed into urban boulevards.

Indeed, trees are a vital ingredient in dense urban neighborhoods. Because residents do not have their own land, so to speak, trees offer a collective yard that can be enjoyed by everyone. No wonder that people dress up trees in winter with strands of lights. Even without leaves, trees can have a magical effect on people and places.

REFERENCES

Hiss, Tony. 1990. *The Experience of Place: A New Way of Looking At and Dealing With Our Radically Changing Cities and Countryside*. New York: Random House.

Wolf, Kathleen. 2005. "Business District Streetscapes: Trees and Consumer Response." *Journal of Forestry*, December.

6

Urbanism and Active Living

Darby Watson, AICP

The United States has a dirty little secret. According to a 2005 report on obesity rates by the Organisation for Economic Cooperation and Development, fully two-thirds of our citizens are overweight or obese. So how did we get so fat? It didn't happen overnight. Obesity is a chronic condition and is caused by a variety of factors. To understand treatments and solutions to this public health threat we need only look to the behaviors and environments that got us this far.

BEHAVIOR AND PHYSICAL ACTIVITY

All of us have an energy balance between our intake of calories and physical exercise that uses those calories. When the intake is consistently higher than what we use, we become overweight. Being overweight or obese is not just an individual problem but a family and community one. Overweight people are at higher risk for heart disease, stroke, diabetes, and hypertension. Obesity hurts people financially and socially. The costs of health care, absenteeism from work or school, and the worry and concern of friends and family all take a toll on the community. When someone has chronic health problems, another family member often will reduce workloads or take time off to care for the ailing relative. This takes a financial toll on the family and the local economy, translating into reduced efficiencies and a strain on the system.

Our eating habits have also taken a turn for the worse, with increases in fat and sugar content in foods; the dramatic growth in preprocessed foods has matched the growth in our waistlines. With our growing girth, we have also developed an enormous diet industry, from imitation sugars and meal programs to drastic surgeries; Americans continue to try anything to lose weight. But are these really solutions? And why would our country have such a problem while others don't? Obesity is a disease of the first world and only we can collectively alter our course.

SUBURBAN DESIGN

Since the end of World War II Americans have moved to suburban neighborhoods in droves. The growth of suburbs has swallowed up forests and farmland at an unprecedented rate. While most of us think of sprawl as an environmental and transportation problem, we often overlook the relationship between sprawl and public health.

According to the *American Journal of Public Health* and the *American Journal of Health Promotion*, suburbanites are on average six pounds heavier than their urban counterparts. This is attributed to a combination of lack of physical exercise and diet. Automobile-based communities often lack sidewalks, crosswalks, and public transportation, all of which contribute to a healthy lifestyle by encouraging walking over driving. Ample free parking is located right in front of buildings. There is no incentive to walk even a few hundred feet between shops, and parking lots can often be dangerous places for pedestrians as drivers circle around looking for that stall just a few feet closer to the front door. Even suburbs with pedestrian amenities often lack a mix of uses that encourage walking.

Low densities mean that services and places of work are located farther away from residential areas, requiring people to drive to meet all of their daily needs. A higher level of density means more services close by and amenities that encourage people to walk to them. Aggregated services located within walking distance also allow land to be used more efficiently by reducing the amount of parking that is needed. Moreover, increased density makes parking in structures, rather than surface lots, more feasible. Generally, a minimum density of 40 units per acre is necessary for structured parking to be cost effective.

The Impact of Suburban Design on Children

Most children no longer walk or ride bikes to school. A recent study in North Carolina showed that more students walked to schools built before 1983 than to those built after. We have made poor site and design decisions that discourage children from walking to school by building the schools on the outskirts of town. Without a safe route to school, many parents have no other choice but to drive. In many suburbs, children take the bus to school even though they live less than a quarter mile from the school. Cul-de-sacs, few connecting streets, lack of crosswalks and sidewalks, and inaccessible school grounds all but require school districts to pick up students by bus.

When children get to school they are often confronted with vending machines full of junk food and school lunch programs that often exceed the recommended levels of saturated fats and sugar content. Many school districts facing budget shortages and rigorous test requirements have cut physical education programs and after-school activities. Many children no longer participate in sports as a regular part of their daily activities, and children are less likely to participate in physical activity without adult supervision. These factors have contributed to a 45 percent increase in overweight children since 1988.

Our children also develop television habits that distract them from playing outside or participating in sports. The average American youth watches approximately six hours of television per day. Add to that the 50 junk food commercials and product placements per average hour of children's programming and you have the recipe for a childhood obesity crisis.

Poor eating habits and low levels of activity are hard habits to break. These habits are often developed even before kids reach school age, as they spend long hours in a car seat to and from day care and other

Television and Health

- A quarter of today's children are obese

- Seventy percent of day care centers use television during some part of the day (www.csun.edu)

- Television viewing rates continue to rise; the average household tuned in for eight hours and 11 minutes per day in 2005 (www.nielsen-media.com)

- Ninety-nine percent of American households own a television

- The latest programming cohort is infants and toddlers

- The average child spends more time watching television than being in school (www.med.umich.edu)

- Three out of four children who are obese when they are 12 years old will be obese as adults activities. Strollers have grown larger and are able to carry older and heavier children, up to 100 pounds in some instances. It's possible to see children up to four and five years old strapped into strollers for a walk through the park instead of walking themselves. Parents often use strollers because they are in a hurry and can't wait for a small child's gait or tendency to wander and explore the world. It's unfortunate that our lives have become busy to the point that it so greatly influences our children's experiences.

Our health is also impacted by the type of work we do. Up until the 1950s many more Americans had jobs that involved physical labor. From agriculture to construction and manufacturing, work was a physical activity. With the rise of the information age, the mechanization of farming, and the growth in the service industry, most Americans do little or no physical labor at work. And yet we are under increasingly high levels of stress and feel busier every day. Workers are in such a rush that they use the drive-through to get fast food for lunch, eat high-calorie foods, and sit at a desk for eight to 10 hours a day.

Our office buildings are often designed with the elevators up front and the stairs hard to find. Many corporations have recognized the

Fig. 6-1. Livable sidewalks allow people to enjoy themselves in the public realm, and walking becomes an integral form of exercise. Source: LMN Architects.

impact of physical activity on health and have instituted programs ranging from smoking cessation to exercise facilities in the workplace in an effort to increase healthy behaviors and reduce health care costs. The classic American city has an urbanized downtown that is mostly offices and businesses that cater to the office workers. This core is ringed with older neighborhoods, then older suburbs that are often deteriorating, and then new suburbs at the fringe. What had been missing until recently were workers living in downtown or close to downtown.

The inner city is often served by public transportation, reducing the need to drive. Encouraging downtown living increases the demand for local goods and services. According to economic rules of thumb, an office worker will support only about one-half square foot of retail, while a resident can support 10 square feet. This 20-fold difference adds to street life, community and civic vitality, and pedestrian potential of the inner city.

Where we choose to live impacts many aspects of our health. Many people drive long distances to work, sit at a desk all day, come home after a stressful commute, eat processed food with high levels of saturated fat, salt, and sugar, and sit in front of the television. Lifestyle choices have reduced physical activity to almost nothing. Even our civic life is suffering. Without people strolling the neighborhood or walking their dogs, without kids walking to school or waiting for the bus, we no longer accidentally run into friends or develop friendships with neighbors. Our lives may be more efficient, but they've lost some richness and diversity that comes from living in an active neighborhood.

OLDER AMERICANS

More people are retired and living longer than at any other time in history. Physical exercise, especially walking, can help people to live longer lives and possibly even prevent conditions like dementia. It helps keep senior adults mobile and independent. As the boomer generation ages, they may benefit from choosing living situations that allow them to walk to their destinations, to shop and run errands without the use of a car, and be an active part of the community and society. Most older adults don't want to feel dependent on others to drive them to activities or be relegated to a facility far from the daily activities of the community. If older adults continue to be included in our communities they can experience a higher quality of life and be engaged in an active neighborhood that supports them as they age.

Certainly, we cannot compel people to move to active neighborhoods with better pedestrian facilities and more services, but we can design new neighborhoods to include these elements so that people can at least have a choice. We can also work to redevelop and retrofit older suburbs to include better amenities and to modify regulations and codes to allow for more infill and more dispersed services and infrastructure to facilitate a healthier lifestyle.

THE LAND-USE/TRANSPORTATION CONNECTION

Increasing levels of obesity have led public health officials to advocate changes in the way we design communities. Though for years urban planners have stressed the relationship between land uses and transportation as a major contributor to our car-based lifestyles, the public health community now recognizes the relationship between obesity and the dependence on the automobile.

By designing communities that encourage walking, biking, and public transportation we are creating healthier communities. A misconception of many urban planners is that people who live in suburban communities simply don't walk. This theory was soundly discounted in Anne Vernez Moudon's study comparing suburban and urban neighborhoods. With comparable residential densities, there were almost as many pedestrians in both communities. One big difference was that most pedestrians in suburban communities tended to be people who didn't have a choice: either they were too young or too old to drive or were new immigrants who didn't have a car. People in urban neighborhoods seemed to walk regardless of age or race, perhaps because the pedestrian amenities are in place for a safe walk and there are services and infrastructure that create a reason to walk.

One of the biggest deterrents to walking in the suburbs is the lack of pedestrian amenities. Sidewalks and crosswalks are often incomplete, are on only one side of the street, or do not lead to where people want to go. Even if sidewalks exist, they often don't cross the large frontage parking lots or have any indications when crossing oversized driveways and drive-through lanes. Blocks and lots are large, often exceeding 600 feet or more per side with little connection between uses within a block. With larger blocks, streets are wider and cars move faster. This makes the motor vehicle paramount. In many suburban communities, grocery stores are required to put up fencing, thick vegetation, or even walls to separate them from residential development. Not only is this unsightly, but the grocery store must constantly repair the barrier. Some customers want so badly to be able to walk next door to get services rather than get in a car that they will tear down fences and scale walls rather than walk along incomplete sidewalks and busy driveways to

Fig. 6-2. Many cities, including Vancouver, are making sure that there are places in downtown for people to walk, jog, bike, and stroll as a part of daily living. Source: Mark Hinshaw.

reach a store the "proper" way. We have solidly given preference in our suburban design over to car drivers to the detriment of walkers and bikers.

Along with the lack of pedestrian amenities, suburban areas tend to offer too much free parking. Small cities and towns will often have no maximum parking limit, so big box stores and malls tend to size parking for the largest shopping day of the year. Free and ample parking is expensive, is an inefficient use of land, causes stormwater runoff problems, and creates poor pedestrian environments. Combine that with the suburban custom of little or no paid street parking and driving becomes the only choice.

DESIGN DECISIONS

Public health is deeply influenced by how we design our cities. By designing small blocks, we encourage people to get around on foot and by other modes in an efficient manner. It may seem counterintuitive, but adding more streets *reduces* the traffic and congestion on all of the streets. Supporting a range of uses, we encourage walking and other nonmotorized modes of travel. Even walking a short distance to a bus stop can have a significant positive impact on health. In addition, a range of day and nighttime uses also supports "eyes on the street" for better safety, reduced crime, and added interest to the pedestrian experience.

Parking meters, pay lots, and commercial garages discourage some people from driving and encourage visitors to park once and walk instead of driving to several destinations. Parking can also be arranged so that several services share a centrally located structure. This lowers costs by reducing parking requirements for each business and creates the opportunity for a more active street by eliminating all the individual lots. Not surprisingly, most inner cities have all of these features.

Many local and regional governments see the growing need for more recreational and pedestrian activities. The Institute of Medicine's *Childhood Obesity Report to Promote Active Living* recommends places to safely walk, bike, and play. The centerpiece of the IOM report is 10 detailed recommendations that form an action plan. One of these recommendations specifically addresses the built environment, citing an urgent need to create activity-friendly community design:

Fig. 6-3. Urban sidewalks, such as this one in Portland, Oregon, should be planted with trees and other vegetation and wide enough to allow for many different recreational activities. Source: Mark Hinshaw.

Recommendation 7: Built Environment

Local governments, private developers, and community groups should expand opportunities for physical activity including recreational facilities, parks, playgrounds, sidewalks, bike paths, routes for walking or biking to school, and safe streets and neighborhoods, especially for populations at high risk of childhood obesity.

Specific strategies to implement this recommendation include:

• **Revise comprehensive plans, zoning and subdivision ordinances**, and other planning practices to increase availability and accessibility of opportunities for physical activity in new developments.

• **Prioritize capital improvement projects** to increase opportunities for physical activity in existing areas.

• **Improve the street, sidewalk, and street-crossing safety of routes to school**, develop programs to encourage walking and bicycling to school, and build schools within walking and bicycling distance of the neighborhoods they serve.

Urban areas offer better opportunities for physical activity. Sidewalks are complete and safe, streets are lined with interesting shops and homes that engage walkers and keep them walking farther. Urban neighborhoods have services and community gathering areas that give people a destination to walk or bike to. Children and teenagers can walk to schools and libraries and this is possible because the density levels in urban areas allow public facilities to be numerous and dispersed to serve all citizens. The recent public health focus on these land-use and design decisions means things are slowly changing. New communities require pedestrian amenities, a wider mix of land uses, and higher densities to encourage more active neighborhoods. Older suburbs are getting remade with new sidewalks, crosswalks, and bike lanes. Communities are infilling with higher densities and mixed uses that bring back the small-town feel and encourage walking, biking, and community interactions that bring vitality back to our neighborhoods.

All communities deserve an environment that encourages healthy living. We all benefit from active communities through better health, lower stress and costs, and a safe, friendly community to share.

7

Density and Children

Areas of cities in or near downtown have been the victims of several decades of disinvestment in "public goods" such as parks and schools. Suburban expansion, white flight, the completion of the interstate freeway system, and low-interest mortgages have all sent financial energy outward to the edges of metropolitan areas.

Therefore, it could not reasonably be expected that households with children would find a commodious and comfortable environment within and near downtowns. Indeed, many adults would not find these settings to their liking, since most people who seek a place to live look for public amenities close by.

But even so, as cities begin to add new parks, libraries, museums, and performing arts facilities into their centers, many people are beginning to consider the center as a definite residential option. Right now, these "urban pioneers" consist of singles, childless couples, and retired and semiretired people who value the convenience, energy, and choices associated with downtowns. These groups are fueling a demand that is steadily increasing in cities and towns of all sizes.

But there is a small but growing minority of households with children beginning to choose downtown and "in-town" locations. Some cities are responding to this by encouraging day care facilities, children's museums, and branch libraries that appeal to families with children. Furthermore, as people from other countries and cultures immigrate to the U.S., they are less reluctant to consider close-in locations and higher density housing.

Interview with a Downtown Mom

Cary Moon is a landscape designer and citizen activist who lives right in the middle of the downtown of a major city. She is the mother of two children: Augie, age 7, and Rusah, age 5. Here's what she has to say about living downtown.

Cary, you have lived downtown for the last nine years, raising two children in that time. This defies the common notion that families can't live in the center, with all the density and lack of green space. What do you say to that?

It is a great neighborhood for kids! My children love the social energy of dense, colorful neighborhoods just like grown ups do. Walking along bustling streets, bumping into familiar neighbors and shopkeepers, seeing the creative energy of city life is fun no matter what your age.

You also do not own a car. I understand that some people are amazed that you can have a "normal" life, doing all the things that parents with children do. How do you do it?

When our first child was on the way, we did consider buying a car. But we realized that we had already figured out simple ways to do the

Fig. 7-1. Cary Moon and her kids prove that contrary to popular myth, families with children can live downtown. *Source: Mark Hinshaw.*

things that other young parents told us we'd need a car for: grocery shopping, doctor visits, etc.—walk or take the bus. I worked in Stockholm for a short time while I was pregnant. Seeing how those urban families did it was inspiring. I saw a family with four kids charging across a busy plaza all on one stroller: two in it, one on the mom's shoulders, and one riding a cool skateboard contraption hooked on the back. Everyone looked happy to be in the middle of all the action. That seemed much more appealing than hassling with car seats and always looking for convenient parking.

Do you think your children are missing anything that is found in more typical urban or suburban neighborhoods?

Happy parents make for happy children. People have been raising kids in cities for centuries, and people all over the world live in tiny apartments—there is no "right" location for good parenting. It comes down to living a life true to our own values—and it turns out kids are pretty flexible. They love being insiders at the local street market. They love taking the bus all over town compared with being strapped into a car seat. They don't mind sharing a room, realizing there isn't much space. They are pretty compassionate and aware of the diversity of human life, as they see lots of different people, including those that are "troubled," every day.

For all the typical kid things, you make do with what's available. We can walk to the aquarium, the children's museum, the science center, and the regular city festivals. We can ride bikes along the waterfront, and play soccer and kickball in the courtyard of our building. When they want to go to a park with a playground, we take the bus.

There is also a fabulous landscaped and secure courtyard where we live which allows the kids to play safely outside.

Many people will immediately mention the absence of schools downtown as a problem with downtown living. What is your view?

Yes, it's true that there is no elementary or middle school downtown, although I believe we are not too far off from seeing that happen, perhaps in a renovated building. My son goes to a grade school that is located in a nearby neighborhood and a bus drops him off a few blocks from where we live. Like many parents concerned with their children's safety, I meet him at the bus. When you think of it, that's not too different from most families with young kids.

MYTHS, MISPERCEPTIONS, AND PROJECTIONS

Several years ago, when I had a regular newspaper column, I wrote a piece about a family who had chosen to live in the middle of the downtown of a major city and raise two young girls. I talked about how the kids enjoyed all of the choices they had within walking distance: several parks, a cultural center with a kid-friendly science museum and an indoor butterfly garden, a large public library, a permanent amusement park, and a lively public market with street musicians and clowns.

I had few of these amenities growing up in a suburban community and, frankly, I thought these kids were pretty privileged. But one reader wrote to me, saddened by the fact that these children did not have their own private yard. She berated me for highlighting children who were so obviously deprived. And she feared that they would grow up missing out on life in a house.

I am sure this woman is not alone in her beliefs. We Americans appear to have forgotten about our long heritage of strong and solid urban neighborhoods where kids grew up healthy and happy playing in parks, vacant lots, and on sidewalks. In fact, many tens of thousands of children continue to thrive in such places that continue to exist in cities like Boston, Chicago, and San Francisco.

Despite the continued existence of these perfectly sound places, many Americans are convinced that the only acceptable environment to raise children is the single-family detached house on its own large lot. This mindset has taken on almost mythic proportions, with people decrying crime, drugs, lack of open space, and other concerns that mark cities as bad places for children.

Safety

There was a period of several decades in which the crime rates in larger cities were indeed significantly higher than in suburbs and small towns. To be sure, in some metropolitan areas that continues to be the case. But in the last decade the incidence of crime in cities has dropped in virtually all categories. By contrast, many types of crime have increased in suburban communities. Even small towns are not immune from serious crimes, in some cases involving children.

In the last several years, many smaller communities have seen tragic and shocking kidnappings, murders, and molestations of children. There have been cases of teenagers shooting other teens in supposedly safe suburban middle-class schools. The fact is, all sectors of our society have settings and situations where children's safety must be looked after. This seems unrelated to the type, size, or location of a community.

Fig. 7-2. The Tashiro Kaplan Artists Lofts in Seattle are in a former warehouse that was converted to housing. Several of the units are occupied by families with children. Source: Mark Hinshaw.

One could even make an argument that denser places offer kids more protection because activities involving children can be organized inside a building. For example, parents everywhere are often fearful of sending their children out on Halloween, given rumors of incidents of strangers handing out candy and fruit laced with drugs, pins, or razor blades. In 2005, the families living in the Tashiro Kaplan Artists Lofts in Seattle sent their children trick-or-treating through the building to neighbors they knew. The neighbors had created amazing costumes and constructions that the kids enjoyed as part of the Halloween tradition.

"We're just starting to mature as a city and as we mature, we're going to see more kids. It's inevitable," said the loft's developer, Cathryn Vanderbrink, in a November 1, 2005, article in the *Seattle Times*. "More young couples who've lived downtown are going to start seeing raising kids here as more of an option."

Family-Friendly Urban Housing

Over the last several decades it almost seems as if there has been a deliberate, concerted, and coordinated effort to make downtowns and neighborhoods around them unfriendly to households with children. The compact, inner city urban school has been replaced by the sprawling suburban school. Small playgrounds and "tot lots" have been supplanted by expansive parks with playfields.

But probably the clincher has been that urban family-type housing has simply been made illegal in most cities. Sometime in the 1950s, most cities adopted zoning codes that set minimum lot sizes at 7,000 to 8,000 square feet. By law, therefore, this eliminated a choice that American families had for hundreds of years: the attached row house.

Typically, these single-family houses occupied lots of 2,500 to 5,000 square feet or even less. They had several floors of living space and a small rear yard or garden. Sometimes there was a space on the ground floor for a tenant or a small neighborhood business, with the latter sometimes operated by the family living above.

The beauty of this type of housing was that people could live in tight-knit neighborhoods with most goods, services, schools, and entertainment within walking distance—*and* own a decent-sized home, albeit on a small lot. What we have systematically taken out of the equation is the small lot.

Despite the absence of any real research indicating that children require large lots to be healthy and happy, we have simply eliminated an entire range of housing choices for American families. And because financial institutions value a house several times more than the value of land, we have also eliminated a potentially affordable housing choice.

Row houses, or town houses as they are sometimes called, are often associated with tenement housing because for several decades around the end of the 19th century both types of housing could be found in the same neighborhoods. Furthermore, in the 1960s and '70s some developers were able to build attached housing using the technique of planned unit development—a technique used by local governments to allow attached housing and denser housing than would otherwise be allowed by zoning codes. The common walls ("party walls") were often poorly built and allowed the transmission of noise between adjacent units. PUDs also forced such housing to be found only in condominium ownership forms, since small, individually owned lots were illegal. Whatever the reason, the row house gained a bad reputation.

But we need to bring it back. We now know how to build to ensure privacy. We have a growing number of households that appreciate urban living. We have families who might wish to include a second unit for a retired parent or a tenant who would help maintain the place and provide a source of income to offset the mortgage.

Clearly we need to change our zoning codes. Row houses should be allowed by right (not requiring a special permit or review) with appropriate standards for height, bulk, and coverage. We must allow a small amount of nonresidential use, so that people can run a small business. Most of all, we need to once again allow small lots.

The row house offers sufficient density—10 to 20 dwelling units per acre—to support local shops, services, and frequent transit, which lower densities cannot. But it does not produce the "stacked flat" apartments that are not as friendly to families with children. This is precisely the density range that has been excised out of most local codes, with the consequence that the only options available to people are very low density or high density. This moderate range is civil, it creates "eyes on the street," and it is of a scale (three to four stories) that does not cause shadows, block views, or overwhelm the street.

We must return the urban row house to its rightful place as a legitimate choice in the housing market.

BRINGING BACK THE URBAN SCHOOL

To some extent, the issue of children and certain forms of schooling within and around downtowns is already changing. More than a decade ago, day care for young children was introduced into downtowns, sometimes in unusual locations such as office buildings.

Fig. 7-3. Vancouver requires a certain proportion of new, high-density dwellings within a project to have three bedrooms in order to encourage families with children to move there. Source: Mark Hinshaw.

What was necessary for this to occur was a change in government standards to allow outdoor play areas to be in locations other than immediately adjacent to the day care center. In many cities today, it is not uncommon to see a line of young children walking along with a long rope-like tether or bunched into little six-seat carriages on their way to a park or a rooftop play area in another building. This kind of reexamination of what were previously considered inviolate standards is occurring in other arenas as well.

Educational institutions used to insist that classrooms be aggregated and packed into exclusively academic campuses. Now community colleges and universities are offering courses within downtowns where they can more easily serve people who also have day jobs. Such locations can also be more easily served by transit. For example, a new rail station on the edge of downtown Everett, Washington, serves commuter rail, intercity rail, and intercity bus riders. The upper floors of the station include classrooms for several academic and job-training institutions.

This same sort of rethinking must occur within primary and secondary education. For far too long, educational building standards have produced expansive, one-story structures, parking lots, and sprawling grounds as the norm—a pattern that can only be created in the suburbs. Yet, even urban schools are held to these idealized, but enormously land-consuming, suburban standards.

Author Constance Beaumont has for several years noted that school districts have been subsidizing sprawl by insisting upon standards that can only be met in outlying locations. She has called for reinstituting the small, urban school model with a compact footprint and multiple stories. She maintains that the traditional model can add to the walkability of neighborhoods, and enhance safety and learning.

Unfortunately, school districts across the country have adopted a one-size-fits-all set of standards that has virtually precluded the traditional urban school that would be ideal for city centers. If we are to have any hope of attracting families with children to the center city, we must revise these requirements or at least allow for greater flexibility based on location.

In fact, we may need to rethink the idea of urban schools altogether and look for locations that are atypical. For example, the Seattle School District operates an "alternative high school" within an old armory structure that is part of the Seattle Center cultural and entertainment grounds. It is tucked into a building that also contains a food court and public meeting spaces. During the day, the students make use of the nearby science center, museums, and the Children's Theatre—a major complex of performance spaces.

Fig. 7-4. This new charter elementary school is located on the edge of downtown Denver in a former bank building. Source: Mark Hinshaw.

For many years, New York City has offered specialized high schools right in the middle of the densest parts of the city. These major multi-story structures offer classes that rival those at the college level and give students access to resources and experiences that would not be available in more scattered locations.

Today in Denver, PS 1 (Public School #1) offers 6th through 12th grade in Denver's Golden Triangle, just south of the downtown core. The school occupies a meticulously restored landmark building that was originally built for a bank. PS 1 is the oldest tuition-free, public charter school in Denver and adds a lively dimension to the center city.

Entirely new forms of secondary education might be tied to community centers or housing developments, blurring the entire notion of school with everyday living to meet the needs of different cultural groups.

PARKS FOR CHILDREN

As with schools, many city parks departments have in the past invested in peripheral locations, with the result that few downtowns offer green spaces. But this is changing as well. Jamison Square, within the central city area of Portland, was designed specifically with children in mind.

Fig. 7-5. Jamison Square, a new urban park in Portland, draws families with children from all over the city. Source: Mark Hinshaw.

Tucked into a single 200-foot by 200-foot block is a large grassy area where kids can play. But the most brilliant element is a water feature that gurgles up successive waves of water that then drain into a basin.

On any given sunny day—and even on some that are not—children scamper about, get soaked, lie in the shallow pool, or lounge on the water-covered rocks. Parents sit nearby on stepped stone walls or benches and chat. On weekends, some families have picnics in this wonderful bit of open space right in the middle of the city.

Older cities such as Boston, New York, and Chicago have long traditions of building parks that accommodate children right within dense urban neighborhoods. They may be small by suburban standards, but they are green and active nonetheless. As with many other elements of our culture in the last several decades, we have confused quantity with quality; we have held fast to the belief that bigger and more is always better.

But that is a false sense of what makes communities work and it may not even be sustainable over the long term given the costs of maintenance, water, and energy. Smaller, thoughtfully designed, and well-managed spaces can serve families with children within urban neighborhoods quite well.

TEENAGERS TOO!

Young men and women need Third Places—places away from both home and school—as much as adults do. A common complaint of teenagers who grow up in the suburbs is that they have no place to go. What they mean, of course, is that there are few places where they can hang out with friends and meet the opposite (or same) sex without close supervision by adults. Typically, they do this in semipublic settings where they can see and be seen. Hence, the suburban mall becomes the only place where they can engage in this kind of behavior—sometimes to the dismay of merchants.

Denser parts of cities, especially city centers, offer teenagers an abundance of places to spend time. There are movie theatres, libraries, coffee houses, shopping streets, parks, plazas, all-ages music clubs, and just plain old sidewalks that are in the middle of the action. Kids have always sought out these places for showing off, displaying their talents, or simply having fun.

But there are also other kinds of places that can be created. In Denver, Ron and Sadie Ben-Ari own and operate an unusual place called Leela. Occupying the street level of an old building located between the 16th Street Mall and the Colorado Convention Center, the place is a combination coffee bar, lounge, and nightclub. During the day, Leela serves espresso, breakfast, and lunch. A bar serving alcohol is at one end of the large loft-like space and a stage and dance floor is at the other. Obviously, people must show IDs to be served drinks.

Leela draws a diverse crowd: construction workers, professionals, "alternative" types sporting tattoos, and kids. The teenagers have a chance to act adult in a place that is both safe and fun. Overstuffed sofas make the place cozy and metal tables and chairs make the place hip. In warmer months, the Ben-Aris put tables and chairs outside, giving Leela a thoroughly European look. Indeed, one wall is painted with a huge version of Van Gogh's well-known painting of a street cafe in France.

THE FALSE PROMISE OF ARCADIA

This country has a long tradition of dense, compact urban neighborhoods, not only in larger cities but in "streetcar suburbs" and even in small towns, in areas close to the main street. Nonetheless, since the middle of the 20th century we have become almost obsessed with the idea that families with children require lots of open, green space.

This is an odd twist on an arcadian utopia where people live in places surrounded by nature so that they may stay in touch with plants and other animals. This notion of living a peaceful, pastoral existence removed from the world has been translated into subdivisions of repetitive builder housing with vaguely colonial or "ranch" details, offering an entirely superficial illusion of living in a rural, untouched area.

The illusion has already been shattered countless times with crime, drugs, and gangs reaching into these supposedly idyllic locations. And, of course, the resulting development associated with low-density living has made everyone dependent on the automobile for every single daily function. In a sense, the technology that brought us freedom and independence has effectively limited our choices.

And so ingrained has this notion of large houses on large lots become that some people have acquired the psychological trait of "projection." Since *they* cannot imagine living any other way, they cannot see why anyone else would want to live differently. This attitude has effectively prevented higher density or even different forms of housing in some communities.

The good news is that this view is gradually crumbling in some quarters. The sheer force of demographic change is causing many cities and towns to reexamine their policies and codes to open up more choices. But we have much work ahead to undo the restraints that were so widely and willfully imposed.

Those communities that have elected to address a broader range of values and needs have found an almost immediate response in the marketplace. Clearly, many people are actively seeking different housing choices and, once again, embracing the idea of urbanity.

8

Public-Sector Investment, Private-Sector Response

Virtually all of the cities that have attracted both new development and new residents into areas within and around their downtowns have distinguished themselves by one salient feature. They have made significant and highly visible investments in the public realm—including streets and sidewalks, public spaces, civic buildings—as well as public transportation.

As David Leland of the Leland Consulting Group, a Portland, Oregon-based firm specializing in urban economics, is fond of saying, "The private sector follows where the public sector leads." It is not enough to simply do plans, adopt policies, or change codes, although doing all those things is certainly important. Rather, the private sector wants to see a city put its money where its mouth is by making and focusing major capital improvements.

In the decades following the Depression and World War II, American cities disinvested in their central cores, either by intent or by neglect. It took several decades to see the effects, but by the mid-1970s many central cities across the United States were dilapidated, abandoned, or eviscerated.

Worse, some cities made attempts at remedies that were weak, misguided, or blatantly classist or racist. Whatever the motivation or lack thereof, the result was downtowns surrounded by "rings" that were barely tolerable as places to work during the day and hardly livable around the clock. This state of civic impoverishment was evident in both physical and social terms well into the 1980s, despite efforts to revitalize many urban centers.

For a number of years, both popular and professional publications were touting the end of downtowns, even suggesting they were unnecessary and dysfunctional relics of a romanticized past. So strong was the drive toward suburbia that films frequently portrayed inner cities as places of hellish nightmares filled with gangs, terrorists, drug addicts, and lunatics. Often even normal residents were portrayed as conniving, sinister, aggressive, or simply neurotic.

In that era, films like *Little Murders* suggested that urban dwellers were randomly executed simply when walking outdoors. Indoor scenes were punctuated by intermittent sounds of gunfire. *The Taking of Pelham One Two Three* was an auditory and visual assault on the viewer (as well as the characters in the story) as thugs hijacked a graffiti-covered subway. Dustin Hoffman's limping, abrasive character in *Midnight Cowboy* was the personification of disfigured and antisocial cities.

PAINFUL LESSONS, FAILED EXPERIMENTS

In order to counter the decay of central city areas, many jurisdictions tried a "silver bullet" approach—a massive, singular action that was intended to turn whole districts around in short order. In spite of many billions of dollars being spent, these efforts rarely succeeded.

Of course, the ravages wrought by urban renewal have been well documented. It was almost as if urban policy was directed to creating ruins like those produced by bombing European cities in World War II, just to have a clean slate to start over again. Sadly, I watched one big city disembowel itself during the 1960s, imploding block after block of grand old art deco era buildings and leaving vacant property that became nothing more than parking lots. Of course, some of these "condemn and clear" projects were thinly disguised efforts to rid an area of minorities and poor people by placing them in concentrated and monotonous housing projects that themselves eventually became unlivable.

Pedestrian malls were invented by architect Victor Gruen, who saw downtowns as needing to mimic suburban shopping malls—a form of development that he helped create in the 1950s. Hundreds of cities shut their main streets to traffic and tried to establish green "oases" among the deteriorated surroundings. Such a fundamental lack of understanding of how cities work and the critical and deeply rooted role of vehicular circulation did little more than hasten the virtual demise of downtowns. Thankfully now, three decades later, most of those cities have "de-malled" their main streets and are seeing commerce return.

It was as if the era of the '60s and '70s was obsessed with recreating downtowns in the image of safe and sanitized, middle-class suburbs. Skywalks became so wildly popular that they were installed in places where climate control—ostensibly their purpose—was not even an issue. So many cities developed this insane rationale for sky bridges: The region was too cold in the winter, or too hot in the summer, or just too rainy.

As William Whyte pointed out in many of his writings, skywalks were simply ways of allowing middle-class consumers to avoid contact with other, less fortunate people in society. And their presence virtually destroyed any street-level activity. No city, even one with very high density, has enough demand to sustain two levels of retail. Accordingly, the street level became even worse. Even today some street-level storefronts are empty or walled over.

Big parking garages—a favorite device of architect Victor Gruen— were built to answer the claim that downtowns did not offer the plentiful and low-cost parking that suburbs did. Today it is impossible to count how many block-long behemoths of stacked concrete dot cities across the country. No salvation was found in such outright ugliness; central cities began to resemble bunkers. Unfortunately, some downtowns, like Denver's, still suffer from the effects of this particular silver bullet, where massive, multistory parking decks loom over too many blocks.

Wide streets and superblocks were popular in city planning and engineering textbooks of the 1950s. Thankfully, the actual implementation of this dreadful concept was seen in only a few cities, mainly those that were not fully formed until the '60s.

Surely one of the worst ideas for downtowns was the "combat zone," an approach developed in Boston for concentrating and, thereby controlling, "adult" businesses. Although other cities might not have used this precise term, there was an era of at least two decades in cities from New York to Baltimore, and from Washington D.C., to Seattle that had almost continuous aggregations of strip joints, X-rated movie houses, adult toy stores, and magazine shops lining many blocks of their downtowns. Even today, San Francisco's Tenderloin carries forward that atmosphere.

Few methods could have been invented to more blatantly discourage reinvestment and revitalization of central city areas. In the last decade, the Internet has lessened the prevalence of this type of business on the street. Some cities have pursued an approach of dispersion rather than concentration. But we simply need to get over our paranoia about such businesses. They are legal and, in moderation, do little harm. In Seattle, an X-rated bookstore continues to operate across the street from a luxury hotel, and a high-end condominium building is about to open directly next door. No one seems to mind.

Finally, the 1980s brought us another silver bullet: the "Festival Market." Advanced by James Rouse for the downtowns of Boston, Baltimore, and New York, it quickly became a must-have for mayors and city councils. Beyond the three original cities, few have been sustained over time. The problem is that these building types often follow a suburban model in that they face inward, only carry national brands, and encapsulate the customer in an environment that could be anywhere. The original urban shopping centers, such as the passages in Paris—some of which still exist today—actually connected parts of the city and were filled with small, locally owned stores. This is a far cry from the branded, sterile, heavily programmed, and policed downtown shopping centers.

All these urban "solutions" have at their core an insidious and intense disdain for cities. They try to encapsulate, sanitize, and suburbanize the public realm. There is no room for messy vitality, spontaneous commerce, and idiosyncratic, homegrown businesses. It's all about mass marketing, market share, and capturing upscale disposable income. Cities that have used these methods have in a sense destroyed their own history and robbed themselves of an authenticity that comes from respecting long-standing patterns and behaviors. In real cities, not everything is tidy. Downtowns have many kinds of people with different income levels and many choices, and some things are simply not photogenic. That is what has always made great cities great. And thankfully, many people are now seeing the value of such places and are voting with their feet and their mortgages.

RESTORE, REUSE, RECYCLE

Cities have always been about renewing themselves, regenerating, and adding layers of richness that comes with time. It is the ability of cities to span centuries and accommodate various waves of architectural fashion that makes them distinct from suburbs.

In my own downtown neighborhood, there are many dignified buildings from the early part of the 20th century, clad in red brick, with stone cornices and intimate courtyards. There is a clutch of tiny, wood-frame houses that date back to a much earlier era. There are tall, sleek towers of apartments and condominiums and squat, glass-covered office buildings. The streets reflect 75 years of trends in building construction and economic cycles. The whole neighborhood used to be an imposing hill that was sluiced down to the bay by a cadre of ambitious and aggressive city leaders. Elsewhere in downtown, buildings that used to hold offices are now used for housing or hotels. Structures that were warehouses now are lofts. A group of row houses is lined with a series of small cafes, taverns, and music venues. What was a car dealership is now a live theater. What had been a big dance hall is now an office building (although it has come full circle in that one tenant now offers ballroom dancing).

My neighborhood is not unique. Similar places exist in every healthy, dynamic downtown. It is not about wiping out and starting over wholesale, but realizing that the buildings and spaces that make up downtown are almost infinitely adaptable with respect to their use. They are containers—some stylish, some not—that can be molded and modified to accept almost any human activity.

Reuse/Recycle in Pittsburgh

Once major retail and residential development in downtown Pittsburgh is complete, three publicly owned buildings in the adjacent Market Square Historic District may also be redeveloped and revived. As Mark Belko of the *Pittsburgh Post-Gazette* reports, the vacant, deteriorated buildings along the Fifth and Forbes retail corridor have caught the attention of the Pittsburgh Downtown Partnership and the Pittsburgh History & Landmarks Foundation. Besides preserving the notable historic facades, redeveloping the buildings would help to revitalize Market Square, an important public place in Pittsburgh since 1784.

The city would sell or lease the properties to the foundation, but ultimately, the proposal's staying power would depend on cost as well as negotiation of the current lease, which runs until 2009. Potential tenants include retail on the ground level and the offices of the Downtown Partnership and others on upper floors. Preservation Pittsburgh, an all-volunteer grassroots organization, has proposed a "transit cafe" in the old Regal Shoe Co. building at Fifth and Market.

One of the buildings had been slated for at least partial demolition due to collapsing floors and walls and an unstable roof. When the foundation stepped in to help pay for repairs, it paved the way toward preservation and adaptive reuse. The foundation does not typically make repairs or assume ownership, but is doing so in this case to allow time for new uses of the buildings to be determined. If they are eventually completed, these reused historic buildings will add a complementary balance to an already evolving high-density corridor of retail, office, and urban residential population.

In fact, it is the public realm that stays relatively constant. Streets and sidewalks, parks and plazas change at a much slower pace. The public realm provides a comparative constancy and serves to temper shorter term change. That is why making sound investments in these common, shared spaces is so important. For too long we have given the public realm short shift when it is precisely the place where our investments matter the most.

The historic preservation movement in the U.S. laid the groundwork for the rediscovery of downtowns. The fight to keep a stock of solid, elegant structures and bring them back to their original glory has ensured that downtowns offer a genuine rootedness of character and ambience that is now greatly prized. Restored train stations, city halls, Carnegie libraries, churches, theaters, hotels, and houses have all contributed to urban settings rich with the patina of time.

Urban Streets and Blocks

Battery Park City in Lower Manhattan was a watershed in downtown development. The plan brilliantly extended the small-scale grid of streets into the landfill site along the shoreline that was created when the World Trade Center was constructed. Previous development plans had suggested massive megastructures—an approach entirely inconsistent with the incremental development pattern of urban centers.

Moreover, the plan rightly insisted that the network of streets, sidewalks, esplanades, and parks would be given the greatest degree of elegance and refinement. By contrast the various housing developments, while dignified, were more background than foreground.

This inspired many other developments in downtowns elsewhere that respected and reflected an urban scale and character.

On the opposite coast, San Francisco's new South Beach neighborhood along the Embarcadero is a wonderful concoction of mid-rise apartment blocks, row houses, cafes, and small parks that look completely comfortable in that city's well-established context. The superblocks-surrounded-by-big-streets approach used in the Yerba Buena urban renewal district was avoided in favor of small blocks and narrow streets.

The north portion of Portland's Pearl District is comprised largely of new buildings. But what roots it firmly in that city is the use of Portland's 200-foot by 200-foot block pattern. The former rail yards might have ended up being a campus-like place divorced from the context. Instead, it already appears to have been there for decades.

Using the existing pattern of streets and blocks of a city accomplishes several things. First, new areas can be seamlessly integrated into older ones. Second, the scale of development is reduced, so that the end result is a more typical ensemble of small parts. Third, each city has a somewhat different dimension to its standard blocks; new increments of development can help strengthen the city's identity. Finally, it allows for many different actors to participate in the development effort with a resulting diversity of form and expression. By contrast, no matter how enlightened a big development corporation is, large-scale developments guided by a singular entity often are repetitive and monotonous.

Parks and Plazas

Open public space has long been a component of great city centers, with origins that go back at least as far as the Renaissance. In the 1700s, the notion of infusing urban cores with great green spaces emerged. Europe's enlightened monarchs, perhaps sensing their eventual demise and wanting to secure their legacies, dedicated swaths of green to public use. Later, as monarchies fell, palatial estates like the Tuileries in Paris became true public parks.

In the U.S., the roots of the tradition of public space being squarely in the center of the city began with the idea of the town green or common. Later, figures like Frederick Law Olmstead and his progeny, the Olmstead brothers, designed numerous great parks and squares in urban centers. Finally the City Beautiful movement solidified this idea of creating grand spaces for the enjoyment of people living in higher density places.

Many fine urban spaces were created in cities during that era, from Rittenhouse Square in Philadelphia to Union Square in San Francisco. But for several decades during the middle of the 20th century, the notion of purely civic urban parks filled with trees and grass seemed to fall by the wayside. Perhaps one factor was that many people began to think of parks as also needing to provide space for organized recreation. Expansive ball fields could rarely be accommodated in dense urban locations where land is at a premium.

But in the last 20 years, many cities and inner ring suburbs have come to realize the critical role that green space plays in making centers livable. In the mid-1980s Yale professor Vincent Scully praised the city of Bellevue, Washington, for building a 17-acre civic green squarely in its center. Today, several thousand people live around the park in high-density housing—a vivid demonstration of the power of green.

Similarly, recent block-sized parks in Portland's Pearl District have made that former industrial district so popular with urban dwellers that developers cannot build high-density projects fast enough.

Fig. 8-1. Rittenhouse Square in Philadelphia is an outstanding example of an elegant, sophisticated urban green surrounded by dense urban development, including housing. Source: Lene Copeland.

Vancouver views urban parks as a fundamental strategy to bring families with children into the heart of the city, a strategy that is enjoying sustained success.

Similarly, San Diego has built a continuous promenade alongside its waterfront street. At points the linear parkway explodes into larger public spaces with unique water features and public art. Maria L. Kirkpatrick, who writes on real estate subjects in San Diego, has noted that the city is in the process of doubling the amount of land devoted to parks in the downtown to more than 90 acres. She suggests that this dramatic investment in the public realm has played no small part in attracting several thousand new households into the downtown, some with children. Six entirely new neighborhoods have been created within and surrounding downtown.

For a period of time, we seemed to be at a loss about how to keep people with antisocial or even criminal behavior from using urban parks. Fortunately, research by the late William H. Whyte and his successor organization, The Project for Public Spaces (or PPS) has given us a new set of tools and techniques for ensuring successful and lively urban spaces.

That work has shown us that ongoing management and active programming are as important as the initial design. We have learned that selling food in public spaces offers a subtle but effective form of monitoring, and that having space surrounded by uses that can keep "eyes" on it throughout the day and night is critical.

The transforming effect of Chicago's new Millennium Park was noted in an article in the June 4, 2006, issue of the *New York Times*. In his piece, "How a Park Changed a Chicago Community," Robert Sharoff observes that the East Loop area, formerly "a sleepy retail and office district—has emerged as one of the city's hottest residential neighborhoods, with more than a dozen projects rising within blocks of the park."

Portland's Public Living Room

The Pioneer Courthouse Square was planned concurrently with the new Metropolitan Area Express (MAX) light-rail system in Portland. The regional transportation management body, TriMet, leveraged funding for transit stops and an information center, which helped to make the Square financially possible. What became "Portland's living room" had extraordinary public support throughout the planning process, including funding from residents. It opened with the light-rail system in 1984, and served both as the city center and the transit hub for buses, light rail, and TriMet's main information center.

The public process surrounding the Square actually started when Portland secured the land, an entire city block, for public use in 1974. Funds were raised by selling paving bricks etched with "owners'" names. To meet the public demands for the space, the modern design by Will Martin was programmed with built-in infrastructure to support a variety of uses. A management entity is now in charge of assuring ongoing effective use of the city park in the form of a nonprofit organization. Pioneer Courthouse Square has a board of trustees that consists of 30 elected members who serve up to two three-year terms.

The Square incorporates public art, flowers, trees, walls, and many stairs, which also serve as seating. There is a permanent coffee shop and other food vendors. Among other permanent pieces of interactive art and culture, there is a small amphitheater facing the steps and a waterfall fountain with a speaker's lectern above. The continued development and success of this public open space is attributed to a continued open dialogue with the community. From the Pioneer Courthouse Square website one can submit a "Place Audit" to rate things such as access and sociability and to give other comments.

Fig. 8-2. The recently completed Millennium Park, with its unique works of art and architecture, has stimulated considerable residential development nearby. Source: Sylvia Lewis.

Sharoff continues, "What has been created there is a mixed use, round-the-clock neighborhood that includes office, residential, entertainment, and open space." He quotes developer Louis D'Angelo, who is converting the former Strauss Building, a 1920s-era office structure with a pyramidal top, into Metropolitan Tower, which will have 243 condominiums: "There's an enormous number of people moving back into the city. Crime is down, the schools have improved, and there's been a huge investment in public infrastructure in the form of new parks and libraries and police and fire stations."

In order to attract people to live in downtowns, cities must return to the important business of funding, developing, and managing public spaces of all kinds—from true landscaped parks to more formal urban plazas. Already the evidence is in: Those cities that have taken this step have seen results in the many new people who choose to live right in the center.

Civic Structures

For most of the history of the United States, we have had a tradition of building fine public buildings. We understood the importance of having libraries, city halls, museums, and schools of the highest quality and greatest prominence. They served as literal landmarks, allowing people to orient themselves in the layout of the town. And they were symbols of civic pride and local democracy at its best.

Over the past several decades, however, we almost lost this tradition. Indeed, we seemed to view public buildings with sort of collective embarrassment. We gave them the meanest of budgets, plopped them down in hidden-away locations, and gave them the most nondescript and spartan forms of architecture. City halls looked like cheap, generic office buildings. Libraries were little more than bloated ranch houses. Schools sometimes were less attractive than industrial parks.

But this sad state of affairs has, thankfully, come to an end in many cities. In fact, some cities have been engaged in a new "golden age" of building splendid, high-profile civic buildings. Libraries are once again regaining their prominent roles on the urban landscape, despite some incorrect predictions that electronic communication would make libraries obsolete. Just the opposite: Urban libraries have become vital community centers, true instruments of learning and socializing.

City halls have started to regain their civic place in communities. Cities and towns of all sizes have built finely designed structures that convey the values of local democracy. Rather than being bombastic symbols of government, these new structures are friendly, accessible, and serve as settings for all sorts of public debate, discourse, and celebrations. After a period of locating government centers in greenfields, they are returning to the center—sometimes in sparkling new structures, sometimes in restored older buildings.

One remarkable trend in the rediscovery of the role of civic buildings is the transformation of the convention center, or as it is called in some communities, the conference center. Once primarily considered a facility for pulling outside visitors in to spend money, these places have taken on both an additional role and a different form. They now serve as venues for a wide range of local events and functions, from flower and garden shows to dances. The Moscone Center in San Francisco, which is largely underground, has movie theaters, museums, parks, playgrounds, and an ice rink on its roof. The Washington State Convention Center includes an enormous barrel vault over the street, which is lined with cafes and contains a living room-like space that is used by local residents.

Schools have yet to rediscover their roles as important elements of urban centers. But this might not be far off. In many cities, older office buildings have outlived their usefulness as places of employment. These buildings could find new life as urban schools.

There are already some promising signs that schools are helping to serve as catalysts for some urban neighborhoods. For example, in San

Fig. 8-3. The roof of the Moscone Center in San Francisco has become a neighborhood hub, with a whole series of connected open spaces and civic attractions constructed on it. Source: Mark Hinshaw.

Diego, the City Heights "urban village" development is a partnership between the city, Price Charities, and City Link Investment Corporation. It includes an elementary school, a Head Start program, and an extension of a community college, along with a gymnasium, a library, park space, and a police station.

Finally, museums are once again becoming vital pieces of city centers. They no longer serve merely as repositories of art for the cultured elite; they have found ways to expand their programs to include a wide range of people with varying ages, incomes, ethnicities, and interests. They often combine with other developments, from commercial to residential, so that their effectiveness as public institutions is enhanced.

Commitment to Transit

For downtowns to be truly livable, a long-term commitment to providing frequent transit service is essential. This allows residents the ability to eliminate one or perhaps all private vehicles. Fortunately, densities associated with downtowns—in excess of 40 units to the acre and as high as several hundred—are more than sufficient to support frequent transit service.

Even bus-only transit service is workable, especially if stops are frequent and buses are reliable. One downside to bus transit is that diesel buses are noisy and produce fumes, effects that detract from livability. To mitigate these impacts, some cities use electric trolley buses while others have purchased buses fueled by natural gas.

Even the design of buses, with low floors that are close to the level of the sidewalk to allow for easy access to the vehicle and upholstered seating, can add to urban livability. And making downtown a fare-free zone gives a distinct advantage to residents. Buses, though not as glamorous as rail, offer great flexibility in service and can respond easily to shifts in density and the emergence of new urban neighborhoods. Boulder, Colorado, has developed a system of buses to serve both the community and the region around it. The compact buses, with low-floor designs, fit better into urban neighborhoods.

Nonetheless, rail transit is a critical element in larger, and denser, cities. San Diego's Red Trolley system has been expanded hand in glove with transit-oriented developments that have "seeded" entirely new

Fig. 8-4. Since the light-rail station was built in San Diego's East Village, numerous residential projects have been built with close proximity. Source: Mark Hinshaw.

neighborhoods like the East Village. Downtown San Diego's phenomenal boom in housing is surely due in large measure to increased accessibility by transit.

Portland's recent addition of a sleek, slender European-type streetcar to its multimodal transit system allows several dense and diverse neighborhoods to be linked together. The streetcars operate within lanes also used by automobiles and trucks and the mutual accommodation has worked well. So quiet is the operation of the streetcars that melodious bells have been added to warn pedestrians at crosswalks of their approach. The overall effect is gentle and serene as the streetcars glide past parks, shops, and stoops.

Intercity rail is also a positive contributor to downtown living because it enlarges accessibility for people who choose to not own cars. Several metropolitan areas, including Chicago, Philadelphia, and New York, have extensive rail systems. Several decades ago, frequent trains

DART and Downtown Dallas

Dallas Area Rapid Transit (DART) moves more than 200,000 people a day across its 700-square-mile service area through a network of light-rail and commuter lines and a fleet of 1,000 buses and vans. Since the 20-mile, 21-station light-rail system opened in 1996, ridership has doubled. In 2,000, voters approved a funding program for light-rail lines to carry another 45,000 riders and for acceleration of an extension to the Dallas/Fort Worth International Airport eight years sooner than planned.

• The $860 million light-rail starter line has generated more than $922 million worth of development—more than a dollar-for-dollar return on the public investment. Property values surrounding DART stations are up 25 percent over similar properties not served by rail.

• Extending DART will cost $1 billion. But as build out progresses, DART expenditures will generate $2.3 billion of economic activity in the Dallas region, and $2.5 billion throughout Texas.

• In downtown Dallas retail sales jumped nearly 33 percent—as opposed to only a three percent rise citywide—from mid-1997 to mid-1998. The in-town apartment market grew from 4,300 units in mid-1997 to well over 9,000 in mid-2000. Prominent national companies like Omincom Group, Blockbuster Entertainment, and the 1,900-room Adam's Mark Hotel, the largest in Texas, cite proximity to DART as the key factor in locating in downtown Dallas.

running between New York, Washington D.C., and Boston became faster and more convenient than flying such short distances. With the time now required for airport security processing, the difference has become even more pronounced.

Other metropolitan areas have followed suit. The Bay Area has an elaborate network of commuter trains serving cities all around San Francisco. Ten years ago, the state of Washington put into service a number of Spanish-made, tilting Talgo trains that allow rapid intercity service between Seattle, Vancouver, Portland, and Eugene.

REDISCOVERING WATERFRONTS

The beginning of the 21st century was marked by a trend that will fundamentally alter the form and function of cities across North America. This is the "recapturing" of waterfronts—whether rivers or bays—formerly dominated by highways, industry, rail, and shipping. Cities are creating astonishing new environments that combine public spaces, civic buildings, and residential uses.

Baltimore initiated this movement two decades ago by converting its old piers to a broad promenade anchored by shopping, museums, and a convention center. But this early effort did not recognize the value of adding housing to the mix. Boston's "Big Dig" replaced an elevated freeway with an underground tunnel, opened up opportunities for parks, and allowed the water's edge and older neighborhoods to reconnect to the city's core. Sites are also being made available for dense residential development.

In Denver, rail lines and associated industries along the Platte River are rapidly being replaced by a tight pack of new streets and blocks lined with housing and shops. A continuous trail is part of this transformation. Likewise, South Beach in San Francisco, and more recently Mission Bay, were former industrial areas now teeming with new development.

A new neighborhood near Jack London Square on Oakland's waterfront has been redeveloped with lofts, apartment buildings, and a dramatic new passenger rail station. The old wholesale produce market still continues to serve as the lively and quirky centerpiece of the district.

Portland replaced its waterfront freeway with a park that has spawned an entire network of shoreline walkways and public spaces, some of which have attracted new housing to their edges; the River District is packed with new housing. Vancouver has redeveloped several formerly industrial areas into vibrant new neighborhoods that mix towers with town houses and waterside esplanades.

Clearly, urban waterfronts are being viewed as a critical element in attracting new residents and new investment. Ports and cities are partnering to transform places where mills and manufacturing once held sway into places that are supremely livable.

9

Re-Forming Regulations

Because downtown areas are also often among the oldest parts of a community, they have been burdened by decades of regulations, some of which can impede or frustrate the development of dense urban housing. One code that I reviewed a few years ago contained over 100 pages, including endless lists of permitted and conditional uses, special districts, tables, charts, cross-references, numerous definitions, and other minutiae that would discourage even the most seasoned of development companies.

In fact, downtown—the very place where we should be encouraging development—is also the very place that likely has the most complex and complicated regulations. There are even cities which, for certain types of projects, require public hearings before the city council. Other cities require onerous permit fees, impact fees, long processing times, or special reviews.

If we are to recast downtowns as places for new investment, we must clean up and in some instances clean out regulations that are outdated, unnecessary, or burdensome.

Regulations have an important role to play as they provide some degree of predictability and convey a community's expectations. But they must also allow prospective investors to quickly determine the potential of developing a particular site without first hiring architects or sifting though numerous city documents. Regulations can, and should be, simple, clear, and easy to read—even by people unschooled in the arcane language of zoning.

We must also seek to make regulations inspirational, not adversarial. Standards should set forth what we want to achieve, rather than assume that we will get the worst and try to do our utmost to prevent it. Regulations should set the bar, and set it high, so that good developers can feel confident that their investment is protected. Indeed, this was one of the original purposes of zoning—to protect land values. In fact, in one community that was seeking to attract private development, a developer demanded that the city put in place design standards before he would move forward with his project.

Most developers see the value in a city having a good, clear set of standards. They don't want to guess about what is potentially allowable. Most are not distressed by standards; rather it is uncertainty in the decision-making process that upsets them the most. If multiple parties need to make a decision and if that decision hinges upon being thrown to the wolves in a public hearing, they will most likely go to another community where the permitting process is more predictable—even if it is more rigorous.

ONE PIECE OF A STRATEGIC PACKAGE

Far too many cities are under the mistaken impression that merely by adopting a plan or changing their codes, they will automatically attract new development. Most developers seek out communities where there is solid financial commitment, not just lip service. And it is not necessarily the case that they are looking for handouts. Rarely will a city simply provide direct monetary assistance. But cities can attract the private sector by financing and building infrastructure and civic buildings as described in Chapter 8.

New regulations and standards must be a part of an overall set of strategies that include capital improvements, tax incentives, and tools such as tax increment financing. One particularly important role that cities can play is in the assembling of property. Cities that have seen immediate results in downtown development have used the acquisition and resale of strategic parcels to "jump-start" new development. Moreover, many cities have found ways to provide structured parking as a part of new development. This alone has often made the difference in making a project feasible. Cities have to be willing to spend money at the front end in order to realize longer term enhanced tax revenues.

IMPORTANCE OF ATTITUDE

Regulations in most communities often make development in peripheral areas far easier to accomplish than within already built-up areas. Most "edge" development consists of single-family subdivisions, strip malls, or office parks that are allowed "by right" and with few (if any) standards. Few groups object to these forms of development and cities are often eager to annex new territory to enlarge their tax bases. So the cards have been stacked in favor of outward, lateral development for several decades.

Trying to do mixed use, multistory development within urban centers is fraught with peril, which increases the degree of risk and uncertainty for developers. Codes are frequently voluminous, with a maze of requirements that are found in different chapters. Some types of development, especially those that need exceptions from the rules, require public hearings and decisions by a city council that can be subject to political forces. Many citizens object to taller buildings and find ways of slowing the approval process. Some jurisdictions require impact statements and impact fees. It's no wonder that many development companies shy away from downtowns.

But some jurisdictions are determined to make it easier to develop within downtowns, where infrastructure is more cost effective, transit service can be supported, and the tax base can be increased significantly above the forms of peripheral development. Many cities are realizing, in fact, that low-rise, dispersed, outward development does not pay its own way and requires substantial subsidies.

Tacoma, Washington, has reduced its previously long code for downtown to about 10 pages—succinct and to the point. Bellevue, Washington, has used traffic calculations to show that urban residential development can be assessed relatively low impact fees in comparison to outlying development.

Portland has a centralized permit counter that allows for coordinated, efficient, and expedited processing. San Diego has decided to be proactive in fast-tracking urban residential projects through the permitting system. Some jurisdictions have assigned special staff to assist in the development process by serving as central coordinators and advocates, ensuring that the process has as few snags as possible.

Urban economist and developer David Leland asserts that the attitude of a city administration can make an enormous difference in whether that city attracts private-sector investment. Development companies appreciate government efforts to welcome them and work in a mode that is more collaborative than regulatory.

Tacoma is so committed to collaboration and smooth permitting that it offers a refund of permit fees if the process takes more than the allotted time. So efficient is its permitting system that no fees have ever had to be returned.

CREATING URBAN RESIDENTIAL DISTRICTS

When the notion of urban, mixed use development started being recognized by cities in the early 1980s, the regulatory response was often to simply create mixed use districts; that is, districts that would allow both residential and commercial development. The trouble with this approach was that property owners pegged the value of their land to commercial use and that meant that the land was priced too high for residential. As a result, few, if any, residential developments were built unless some form of subsidy was involved.

A more effective approach is to create districts in which a mix of uses can occur, but to "weight" the potential substantially in favor of residential uses. This approach clearly signals the city's intent and keeps land prices in line with normal land cost/unit cost ratios for residential development. It also prevents landowners from speculating on the prospect of someone cashing them out to build an office tower.

Sometimes, this might require rezoning an area to realign the property values. Cities that have done this have seen results in that the land supply is shifted towards residential use. Some property owners have resisted this, claiming downzoning, but in fact have actually been able to sell their properties faster.

An irony now in many cities is that urban residential development is now outstripping office development. As the economy shifts away from concentrations of high-rise office towers (in a sense, the factories of the late 20th century), land is becoming more valuable for residential use. This is being seen both in new development as well as in the adaptive reuse of older Class B and C office buildings into apartments, condominiums, and hotels.

Finally, while there will certainly be some people who embrace the idea of living right within a financial district, most residents of city centers will look for places with a true neighborhood ambiance. In a sense, people seek the same attributes in urban neighborhoods as they do in conventional neighborhoods: quiet at night; neighborliness; local shops, services, and cafes; safe streets; and eyes on the street. Accordingly, cities need to carve out districts that are predominantly residential but allow an abundance of other choices as well.

SIMPLIFYING CODES

Land-use codes need not be as elaborate and convoluted as many, unfortunately, seem to be. Part of this length comes from long and detailed lists of uses, which will be addressed below. But design standards also contribute to lengthy codes. Portrayed in code form, design standards seem drained of their intent—as if it were possible to quantify good design.

What cities should do is boil quantitative requirements down to a bare minimum and place provisions that address the quality of development

Fig. 9-1. Denver's commercial core is now ringed with several dense urban neighborhoods, many of them in former parking lots or vacant buildings. Source: Mark Hinshaw.

into a separate document. This should, of course, be adopted into the municipal code by reference, so it has the force of law behind it. But once these qualitative elements are stripped out of the basic code, it should be possible to capture all the provisions that a developer needs to know within a handful of pages.

Essentially, the hard-core code for a downtown need not consist of more than the following subjects. The precise numbers might vary among different districts depending on their purpose, but nonetheless it should be possible to convey the pertinent information in a few easy-to-read charts.

Uses

Because the nature of downtowns is that they can embrace virtually any type of function, it is counterproductive to have a long list of permitted, conditional, and special land uses. If properly crafted, design standards should be able to mitigate the effects of most uses if they are fully contained within structures. And if the downtown has been planned to identify infrastructure needs, individual uses should not have to "prove" that they can be accommodated.

USE LIMITATIONS
All uses shall be allowed, unless prohibited below.

Prohibited:
- Adult Establishments
- Billboards
- Drive-Through Businesses along Pedestrian-Oriented Streets
- Gasoline Service Stations
- Industrial Uses
- Mini-Storage on the street level.
- Outdoor Sales or Rental of Boats, Vehicles, or Equipment
- Outdoor Storage of materials and equipment (except during construction)
- Repair of Vehicles, unless entirely within a building
- Sewage Treatment Plants
- Surface Parking on Pedestrian-Oriented Streets
- Work Release Facilities
- Wrecking Yards
- Vehicle Washing, unless located within a building or parking structure
- Any other use that the Planning Director determines not to comport with the intent of the district.

Fig. 9-2. Having a concise list of uses that are not allowed in a downtown can be more effective than a long list of allowable uses. Source: LMN Architects.

Instead, a city could determine a short list of uses that it would not want to have within downtown under any circumstances because they would not contribute to its safety, liveliness, or appeal. Heavy industry is one likely category, as would be open storage lots and maximum-security prisons. Each community may well determine that certain additional uses, such as drive-through businesses or gasoline service stations, are incompatible with the long-term vision—at least for certain districts. This short list of prohibited uses should ideally fit into less than a single page of text.

Floor Area Ratio (FAR)

It has recently become popular for advocates of "form-based" codes to recommend eliminating the tool of Floor Area Ratio in favor of bulk and dimensional standards. While this approach may be valid in low-rise areas, it is not logical to apply to high-density, high-rise, mixed use downtown districts. This blanket dismissal of a completely appropriate tool is misguided for several reasons.

First, the development community—not only within the United States, but internationally—uses Floor Area Ratio as an indicator of the development potential of a site. It is a simple calculation that does not require an architect to figure out what can fit within a bulk envelope. In fact, when a developer first looks at a downtown parcel of property, the first question usually is, "What is the allowable FAR?"

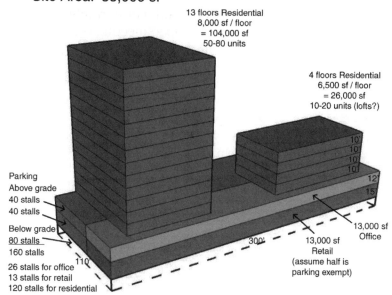

Residential over Office over Retail
Site Area: 33,000 sf

13 floors Residential
8,000 sf / floor
= 104,000 sf
50-80 units

4 floors Residential
6,500 sf / floor
= 26,000 sf
10-20 units (lofts?)

10'
10'
10'
10'
12'
15'

Parking
Above grade
40 stalls
40 stalls

Below grade
80 stalls
160 stalls

26 stalls for office
13 stalls for retail
120 stalls for residential

110'
300'

13,000 sf
Office

13,000 sf
Retail
(assume half is
parking exempt)

Fig. 9-3. As a tool, Floor Area Ratio allows a mixture of uses while setting basic level of intensity that a city considers appropriate. It also allows for a bonus system to be used. Source: LMN Architects.

FAR offers a degree of predictability and certainty. But beyond that it is a very useful tool. It allows for mixing uses by specifying the outer limit of intensity, but not specific densities, as the tool of dwelling units per acre does. In fact, density as expressed in dwelling units per acre carries with it a built-in incentive to build larger units. There is no advantage to building smaller units, since the yield is identical. With FAR the developer decides the size and mix of units. With FAR, the smaller (and more affordable) the units, the more can be built.

But FAR also allows flexibility as well. Form-based codes seek to attain a degree of uniformity in urban form through dimensional standards. Uniformity is antithetical to vital, diverse downtowns that thrive on a variety of form, height, style, and appearance. FAR allows almost an infinite range of building forms from smaller, low-height structures to towers. It allows development to be a function of parcel size and therefore automatically produces variety.

FAR also allows a jurisdiction to weight the development intensity in favor of certain uses, like residential. For example, FARs for residential use can be set higher for a particular district to ensure that it is predominantly residential.

FARs can be used with a bonus system that rewards developers for including certain amenities within a project—amenities that would not otherwise be available to a neighborhood. For example, day care could be a bonusable feature. Or a neighborhood meeting room. Or public art. A public facility like a branch library could be on a list of items to receive bonuses. In return for including such features, a developer would be granted additional FAR.

FARs can also be used to help retain historic buildings, many of which are far below the development potential set by code. By allowing a transfer of FAR to other sites, the owner of the historic structure is compensated for keeping it in perpetuity. No public funds need be involved, as this can be a purely private transaction.

FAR, along with bonus systems, has been in use in larger cities for several decades. It is well established and has met the test of court challenges. As a tool for regulating downtown growth and development, FAR is now being used in mid-sized and smaller communities. It continues to be a useful and appropriate regulatory technique.

Height

It sometimes seems like nothing can get neighborhood groups more agitated than the thought that a "tall" building might be built in their vicinity. Of course, height is relative, along with its perception. I once worked with a community in which there was a long and raging controversy over whether to allow building heights in downtown to be increased from 30 feet to 33 feet—a difference of *three* feet! Many vocal citizens were fearful that the increased height would allow "high-rises." Entire public meetings, filled with acrimonious testimony, were devoted to this issue alone.

In another community, a suburban one that was maturing rapidly with urban intensities, activist neighborhood groups appealed a high-rise building in a court case that took five years and ended up in the state's supreme court. Their claim was that taller buildings were destroying the "rural" character of the community.

From one perspective, it could be argued that once a city allows high-rise, multistory buildings, what difference does it make whether they are 14 stories or 40 stories? But apparently to some it does. In the early 1990s, voters in both San Francisco and Seattle handily passed initiatives that placed limits on the heights of downtown towers.

So despite the preference on the part of the development community not to have height limits in a downtown, it is an inevitable standard. Part of the psychology, perhaps, is that people simply don't like being taken by surprise. In one city, a creative interpretation of a zoning code gave one developer an extra 25 stories and produced a looming structure that even today is widely derided.

It is useful to consider height limits, especially ones that can be pegged to other codes and industry standards. It does little good, for example, to have a height limit of, say, 90 feet when the building code requires considerably more construction costs for any building over 75 feet. The higher cost cannot be recovered by simply adding a few stories. In fact, it would be smart for cities to coordinate height limits imposed by zoning with important "break points" in the building code. Now that many cities are adopting International Building Code (IBC) this should be easier to accomplish.

For example, 40 to 50 feet of height is a break point for wood frame construction. Higher than that, and more costly building methods are necessary. Another break point is 75 feet, because above that true "high-rise" construction codes are triggered. Once into the high-rise category, there is a minor change at around 160 feet, but beyond that there are not significant break points—although there may be other rationales that make sense. For many years, for example, Philadelphia did not allow buildings to exceed the height of the statue atop City Hall. Washington, D.C., uses the height of the Capitol dome as the maximum. In one city surrounded by tall evergreen trees, the mature height of those native trees was used as the limit.

San Diego requires calculation of sun angles and shadows to determine height, although this requires modeling rather than making a limit clear at the outset. San Francisco limits the height of buildings that would potentially shadow certain designated parks. Seattle and other cities impose setbacks over a specified height along designated "view corridors" to ensure that a key aspect of community character is protected.

A number of communities have adopted a "stair-stepped" zoning envelope for downtown as a whole to create a particular effect or to reinforce topography. Some cities have Height Overlay Districts that tailor building height or setbacks to certain conditions, such as the proximity to low-rise neighborhoods or to relate to the scale of historic buildings.

Building height is clearly an issue that needs to be addressed in codes for downtowns. Both developers and citizens expect some predictability.

One interesting trend in the discussion of building heights relates to the growing number of high-rise residential projects in many cities. Vancouver can be credited for advancing a regulatory concept that allows for greater height if the bulk (as expressed in "floor plate" size) is decreased. In the last five years, that city has seen the emergence of a very distinctive, "pencil-like" residential tower—very slender (with floor

Fig. 9-4. For a number of years Vancouver has encouraged taller but very slender "pencil" towers to allow light to reach the street and public spaces. The result is also a more graceful skyline. Source: LMN Architects.

plates less than 7,000 square feet) but very tall. Ostensibly, this allows for views between buildings (Vancouver also has a regulation for tower spacing distance) and a pattern of development in which very tall towers are surrounded by an "understory" of row houses. The combination of sleek, glassy towers with sidewalk-hugging homes is not only striking but adds immeasurably to the sense of street life.

Fortunately, we now have computer models that can depict the effects of different building height limits and to, in a sense, "sculpt" the skyline. Maps with numbers never could adequately convey the three-dimensional aspects of development. Now we can see it in advance and discuss the merit of different approaches.

Parking

Of all of the subjects associated with regulations for downtowns, perhaps the least glamorous and exciting is that of parking standards. Yet parking is probably as much a determinant of development intensity as any other factor. Developers depend on it in order to get financing. Cities carefully review and monitor the provision and use of parking. For better or worse, the supply of parking has driven the form and location of development.

Over the last two decades, Robert Cervero of the University of California, Berkeley, has researched the effect of parking on development and on behavior. He has suggested that cities should use parking ratios strategically to create compact, walkable, transit-oriented development.

He has advocated that communities apply maximum parking standards, rather than minimums. His studies show that it is possible to change patterns of commuting by making parking in short supply. He has documented this effect in a number of cities that have adopted this policy direction. And most of these are in suburban locations where constraining the supply of parking has actually led to *more* development.

After all, developers often cannot charge the full cost of parking, especially in suburban locations. They often embrace the notion of limiting parking because it reduces their costs. So long as a jurisdiction provides options, such as transit, carpools, or vanpools, employees will eventually rearrange their lives. Doing without parking is not the end of the world.

In fact, downtowns with constrained parking supply often enjoy greater retail activity. This is because constraining supply produces a classic market mechanism of increasing the price. Once the price is high enough, people will choose to park once and then walk to multiple destinations, whereas if they can easily drive and park cheaply, they are likely to only conduct one piece of business. In some ways, the high parking requirements found in many codes also contribute to traffic congestion, because consumers make series of short trips between destinations.

So it is very useful for cities to consider crafting parking standards to reinforce patterns of behavior that discourage the movement of cars. Moreover, when the price of parking becomes too high, people will elect to use transit. There is nothing like a direct hit to the wallet to alter human behavior.

Here is a dramatic example that occurred in one city a number of years ago. City employees drove their own cars and parked for free in the large lot surrounding the building. This had been the pattern for many years, despite the city's expressed policy of encouraging alternative forms of transportation.

One day, after the development community chided the city for not following its own policies, the city manager announced that beginning the following month, employees would have three choices. They could continue to drive and would have a parking stall. But $40 a month would be deducted from their paychecks, a figure that would be at least double in today's money. Or they could sign up for a carpool and nothing would be deducted. The third choice: They could take the bus and $40 per month would be *added* to their paycheck.

Of course, the manager soon had a revolt on his hands. Letters of protest poured in. Some employees threatened to form a union. People moaned and groaned and defiantly said they would continue to drive.

But the manager held fast. Three months later, the mode split (High Occupancy Vehicle Use) went from around five percent to nearly 40 percent. Everyone made their selection and simply rearranged their daily schedules. No one quit and life went on.

So parking can indeed be a powerful tool.

It is also necessary to make sure that dimensional standards reflect urban conditions. In tighter, more compact development, it is senseless to require stall widths and lengths that are like ones applied to suburban parking lots. Fitting what parking is provided into dense urban buildings means smaller, more efficient stalls.

DESIGN STANDARDS AND GUIDELINES

Having a good set of design standards and guidelines is important to directing the character and quality of downtown development. These provisions should not be prescriptive but rather allow for great latitude in meeting their objectives. Each design standard and guideline should clearly state an intent, so that if other solutions are proposed, they can be evaluated against the intent. The determination to allow other solutions should be based upon whether it is meeting the intent, or ideally, exceeding it.

Just as the basic regulations should concentrate on a short list of subjects, so should design standards. If they are too lengthy and complicated, their proponents can get discouraged. Some of these proponents will not be large development companies with decades of experience in

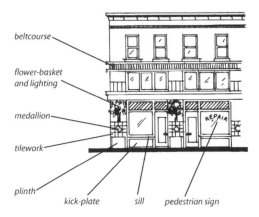

Fig. 9-5. It is important for cities to adopt standards that describe the expectations for new development visually and verbally, especially at the street level, to avoid blank walls or austere facades. Source: LMN Architects.

downtowns. Some will be small, locally based, and not necessarily familiar with the state of the art in regulations.

Accordingly, standards should be written in plain English with short declarative sentences. If technical terms are used, they should be defined in a glossary. The overall attitude expressed by the standards should be to inspire people to do good work, not merely to toe the line with adherence to numerical details. For the most part, standards should be expressed in descriptors. If numbers are used, they should be in ranges, to allow for built-in flexibility.

Within downtown settings, standards and guidelines should generally focus on the street-level environment—the setting that has the most impact on the public. The upper levels of buildings can be left to the discretion of the private sector, except in cases where the tops of buildings can have an effect on the skyline. In the latter case, there may be a few standards that address shape, concealing communications or mechanical equipment, or lighting. But it is the first few levels of a building, where it interacts with the public realm, that should receive the bulk of attention.

The Base

New downtown development often takes the form of a taller part of a building rising up from a lower base. The base can include commercial uses, parking, or both—although parking should generally not be allowed to directly abut the sidewalk without an intervening use. It is important to make sure that the base contributes positively to the experience at the street level—not just directly in front of the building, but as seen from across the street and down the street.

Many cities subject the base to "set-to" lines or maximum setback lines. In some locations, additional sidewalk width is desired, although it is possible to go overboard with this. Rarely, even in very intense downtowns, do sidewalks need to exceed 20 feet in total width. In most cases a 14- to 16-foot width is perfectly adequate to allow for pedestrian movement. There are examples of needlessly wide sidewalks that seem vacant most of the time.

The appropriate height of the base is a factor worthy of consideration. This might be based on the long-standing historic pattern of development to allow newer buildings to better fit into the context. Often downtowns have an "understory" of buildings that are in the range of two to six stories. Alternatively, the base height could be related to the street width. Most downtown streets are 60 to 90 feet wide and a ratio of 1:1 (wall height to width of street) seems comfortable.

Streetscape Envelope: The Horizontal Dimension

There is a linear envelope of space that hugs the lower, outer edge of urban buildings as they front the adjacent sidewalks. This envelope has a vertical dimension of approximately 15 feet and a horizontal dimension that is similar. This represents the public realm and it contains a host of elements that address sociability, safety, and visual appeal. The components and characteristics of this sidewalk space are discussed in Chapter 5.

THE VERTICAL DIMENSION: THE STREET WALL

The most important aspect of the wall that immediately abuts the sidewalk is its richness of visual interest. Blank walls are deadly in any downtown and some cities, unfortunately, abound with them.

The main culprit is parking structures. No parking garage should be permitted to present a blank wall—or (arguably) worse, an open bay of parking to the street. Ideally, the sidewalk level should contain shops; at a minimum, retail space can be inserted into the corners, which are not efficient for parking anyway. If retail space is not provided, a whole host of other measures can be taken, from landscaping to decorative grillwork to artwork. One solution that is often proposed but almost never works is vines that are intended to grow up a wall. Urban conditions are too harsh to allow vines to flourish (with the possible exception of tropical settings).

But beyond parking structures, retail and services can play a key role in enlivening the street wall. Retail is not always necessary; indeed, there might not be sufficient demand for it everywhere. So it is important to establish a hierarchy of streets, with some requiring retail uses (usually a minimum percentage of frontage length) to varying degrees. Street-level office space should not be allowed to substitute for this, as occupants will likely use blinds for privacy, thereby creating another kind of blank wall.

When retail uses don't make sense, a city can require other features. These can include murals, display panels, bas-relief, masonry patterning, unique lighting, and other permanent, physical enhancements.

It is worth noting here how the use of ground-related housing can enhance downtown streets. In recent decades, this has become almost a lost art. But some cities are rediscovering its useful role. Vancouver, for example, requires street-level row houses in certain areas, and requires that they be set back several feet (and raised up several feet for privacy) to allow for shallow planting areas, steps, and stoops. In some developments, small gardens decks have even been added. These little

Fig. 9-6. Many elements make up successful retail frontage. These are essential to making livable downtown streetscapes. Source: LMN Architects.

spaces can add eyes on the street. One can be walking along streets in Vancouver and suddenly be aware that people are having breakfast a few feet away. This semiprivate "front yard" is a classic device seen in older cities such as Boston, Philadelphia, and Baltimore. Cities should find ways to encourage them in downtown neighborhoods.

In commercial areas, the street wall should have windows for a high degree of transparency. Their dimensions should be generous and create an appearance of storefronts. In this regard, the sill height is an important detail. It should generally be between 24 and 30 inches. Lower than that, it has an office look; higher than that, it is more like a typical window than a storefront. It is ironic that codes now need to specify this dimensional detail, which has been a successful rule of thumb for decades, but which is, unfortunately, absent from many contemporary buildings.

Beyond these few elements, it is only necessary to consider a few additional things that could reflect regional or climatic conditions. For example, are awnings or canopies warranted? (This does not include arcades, which are almost never successful and can actually deaden a street by placing shops back into deep shadows and setting up a line of columns that obstructs visibility.) In some regions, certain materials like limestone are often found on the lower levels of buildings. Each city should consider elements like this that help reinforce its character, history, or location.

PROCEDURES

Ministerial Permitting

Many cities attempt to accomplish goals for downtowns through their normal permitting process. This assumes that good places can be developed using a cut-and-dried set of regulations, in which numerical specifications eliminate all chance of variation. This is usually a mistake, as good cities are not built by numbers. Nor do most developers prefer this process, as buildings often have individualized requirements.

It is far better to establish a good, open, fair, and expeditious design review process that can allow for flexibility, interpretation, and collaboration. This can allow the public sector and the private sector to "tailor" individual development projects to particular sites. Used properly, the result can be more diverse and satisfying to all.

Design Review

The subject of design review is complex. To conduct this process in a manner that is efficient and legally defensible requires careful thought. Both administrative design review forms and those involving appointed boards must follow principles set forth in case law, as well as in enabling legislation.

Readers should refer to publications such as those the American Planning Association's Planning Advisory Service offers to ensure that these procedures are appropriately crafted.

STAFFING

A final factor in ensuring the success of downtown living is the role that key staff people can play within local government. The most successful cities have usually had at least one individual who was a "champion" for downtown residential development.

Sometimes this has been an economic development official. Other times it has been a management level planner. And in other cases, it has been an urban designer. In a few cases, architects working within city government have been persistent advocates.

This person must be able to bridge many areas of expertise and gain cooperation from various departments and other agencies. The person must have a working knowledge of zoning and building codes, financing methods, permitting processes, funding sources, and public works standards, and also be adept at citizen involvement techniques. The person must also display political acumen and be well regarded by elected and appointed decision makers.

Sometimes, this function can be taken on by a committee of staff people. But it is important to have people whose job description includes these responsibilities and charges. Often, it all comes down to people engaged in conversation and persuasion.

10

New Imperatives for a New Era

As we move into the next several decades, it is clear that the aging of the baby boom generation will have a profound effect on the form and function of communities. Whereas many people in the generation prior to the boomers were content to live out the last years of their lives in retirement communities or alone, the preferences of boomers will be much different.

In fact, it is perhaps the first time in the history of North America that two demographic groups are seeking virtually the same thing. Many people in their mid-50s and mid-60s (aka baby boomers) and people in their 20s want to live in places where they are surrounded by lots of "cool" choices: arts, culture, entertainment, food, shops, recreation, and simply places to hang out, such as bookstores, coffee houses, and cafes.

One might conclude that boomers simply want to live like they are young again, but it is likely that their desires go deeper than that. In many unprecedented ways, the baby boom generation, especially women, had many opportunities not available to previous generations. Higher education, mobility, travel, and satisfying work were all facets of life assumed to be easily attainable. It is understandable that this group—one that will live longer than any population group in history—will seek to extend those choices into their older years.

Just as the baby boomers affected education—primary, secondary, and higher—for a period spanning three decades, their effect on the structure of cities and the provision of goods, services, transportation, and transit will be dramatic and far-reaching. From a purely market perspective, the impacts will derive from the huge amount of both equity and disposable income held by this group. But from a social perspective, the preferences will demand many new responses from the private sector, government, and institutions.

The following "soft" predictions are intended to suggest the range and scope of some of these changes.

TURNING PARKING LOTS AND OFFICE BUILDINGS INTO HOUSING

This is not very farfetched, because in some places these phenomena are already occurring. In many cities, where land values have increased significantly in the last decade, it no longer makes sense to waste land for asphalt and parked cars. In a sense, the pattern of land development since the middle of the 20th century has produced a de facto "land bank" in which urban sites can be transformed from parking to places to live. In some cases, this means literally tearing up lots and adding housing in their place. In others, it means tearing down an existing low-rise structure—a box surrounded by asphalt—and rebuilding a new form of development. In many communities this has taken the form of

Fig. 10-1. Supermarkets, such as this Safeway in Seattle, are beginning to be part of residential projects. Source: Mark Hinshaw.

Living Over Your Groceries

Seattle architect Mark Simpson designs buildings that contain homes on top of supermarkets. Simpson is a passionate advocate of this unusual form of mixed use. He cites numerous benefits to the urban community, including social interaction. Residents living over and near the store frequently shop on foot, resulting in familiarity among neighbors. Because they are open both early and late, the markets generate active streets and sidewalks that provide safety and security to the neighborhood.

Because many shoppers walk, bike, or take the bus, no huge parking lot is needed and there are fewer impacts generated by auto use. Simpson estimates that, if the 180 residents living on the upper floors of the architect's project each make three trips a week to the store within their own building, as many as 540 car trips are eliminated.

Simpson asserts that urban supermarkets will be successful when they are attractive and convenient to people who do not need to drive. His mixed use projects offer weather protection to pedestrians on the sidewalk as well as a few intimate outdoor seating areas. Additionally, a grocery store as an anchor tenant often attracts a number of smaller tenants.

Challenges include downtown zoning and design regulations that can complicate the receiving, distributing, consuming, and selling of products. The typical suburban model involves a flat site. Urban sidewalks and streets are often sloping, which constrains the location of store entrances and loading areas. Furthermore, when building additional floors above, there are potential inefficiencies with elevators, stairwells, and the location of mechanical systems. All of these issues can be worked out in the design. However, Simpson notes that if a retail space is not initially designed for a grocery store, it is almost impossible to retrofit one later.

multiple stories of housing on top of a supermarket on a site that previously might have held a conventional stand-alone grocery store.

In Seattle, there have been at least a dozen such developments since the year 2000. And some have gone well beyond the initial model of housing over a market. In one case, a large, upscale supermarket has been tucked almost entirely underground, with a small but prominent street entry and multiple levels of parking. Rising above are three towers, one containing a hotel, two containing condominiums. And the whole complex surrounds a central urban square. What had been an old manufacturing plant and lots of surface parking on the edge of the city center is now a new, dense, mixed use development that will serve as the focal point of an entirely new, rapidly emerging neighborhood.

Another unexpected turn of events is that many cities have an inventory of modest but nicely detailed office buildings, most of which were constructed in the 1910s and 1920s. These early deco-era structures have small floor areas, too small for contemporary office layouts. So they are gradually being converted into solid, elegant apartments and condominiums, or in some cases, boutique hotels. As places to live, these wonderful buildings can continue to provide a richness of character to city centers.

I suspect that this trend will perhaps even extend to office buildings built in the '50s and '60s, as many buildings of that era were also small. There might be a new life for many early modernist buildings as even that era is appreciated for its unique style.

It is fascinating to realize that we have gone so far beyond the original goals of historic preservation. Rather than being trashed, buildings of widely different eras are now being valued for entirely new economic uses. This attitude of recycling instead of removing is one that also reflects new thinking regarding sustainability.

URBAN COTTAGES AND COMMUNITY HOUSING

One of the difficult decisions for many people to make is to move out of a house they have occupied for many years, especially one where they raised their children and that they spent long hours giving loving care and attention to. But at some point, interests change and what was a joy becomes a burden. Yet the very thought of locating in a "retirement" center makes many people distraught because it signifies a loss of independence and isolation. Furthermore, many people have become used to the idea of living in a house that is freestanding; somehow the idea of living in the same building with neighbors suggests giving up privacy and control. So we are beginning to see new forms of housing being devised to meet the needs of people who want to downsize but still maintain independence and a sense of individual ownership.

"Cottage housing" developments have been put together as a response to this change in the marketplace. Cottage houses are very small houses—1,000 square feet or less—either on small lots or on land owned in common. The cottage might have a basement and two floors, giving it a small footprint in the range of 300 to 400 square feet.

One developer, The Cottage Company, even offers model codes for jurisdictions to adopt to allow this form of development in areas otherwise zoned for single-family housing. The result is often several cottages in place of one huge house. The idea is that because the cottages

Fig. 10-2. The new Metropolitan Tower residential development in Chicago is in the former Strauss office building, once the headquarters of Encyclopedia Britannica. Source: Sylvia Lewis.

are small, the number of occupants is limited. They therefore have much less impact than large homes in terms of traffic, soil displacement, drainage, etc.

But their main advantage is that they are high-quality houses that are very efficient and compact. "There is a vast, untapped market for this form of housing. We can't seem to build them fast enough—so long as cities permit them," says Jim Soules, owner of The Cottage Company. Indeed, Soules is building the "Lexus" of housing: compact, beautifully handcrafted, and very comfortable.

Cottage housing is an idea whose time has come. It is an ideal form of urban housing for leftover, infill locations within close proximity of city centers.

By the same token, there is a small but growing demand for a different type of community housing, often called cohousing, which is patterned after similar efforts in Denmark and other Scandinavian countries. This arrangement contains a number of small units: some within a larger structure, others attached, and perhaps still others detached. The land might be owned in common and there are shared facilities such as a workshop, meeting and party room, and a shared kitchen for community events or meals. The residents own the housing and the land and are responsible for the maintenance of common areas, usually taking on the responsibilities themselves.

However, cohousing is not for everyone, due to its social structure and the fact that it requires a long-term commitment during financing, design, and construction.

In the coming decades, we will see many new forms of community housing that allow people to share aspects of living. These will also involve complex social mechanisms in which some residents might be caregivers to others or simply take care of children while other adults are at work. This is not unlike home-sharing, but on a larger scale.

EQUALIZING HOUSING CHOICE: ELIMINATING THE TAX BREAK

American home owners have viewed the ability to deduct the interest on their mortgages from their income tax as some kind of basic entitlement. However, this incentive to own a house is less than 80 years old. It was first put in place to benefit the middle class and allow them to secure a stable investment.

Since then its use has been expanded such that a large number of citizens use the tax break to buy second homes. Moreover, the tax break disproportionately benefits the owners of large, very expensive houses.

Fig. 10-3. The Dearborn cohousing project is close to downtown Seattle and offers families the opportunity to pool their financial resources and be their own developer. Source: Pyatok and Associates, Architects.

It can be argued that by giving large tax breaks to wealthy individuals, the tax burden has actually been shifted back toward the middle class—certainly to those who rent.

Ironically, many of those who decry the use of government policy for "social engineering" seem to have no problem with this immense subsidy of consumer behavior. It is not only one of the largest forms of subsidy given by the federal government, but it has, in fact, been a massive example of social engineering, fueling outward expansion of urban areas and the resultant massive expenditures of local dollars to service and maintain the outward expansion.

And while such a subsidy benefits people on an individual basis, it is grossly inefficient on a collective basis. Many studies have documented that low-density, single-family development does not support services by its tax revenue. Indeed, some communities are loathe to annex purely residential development because it increases expenditures but not revenue.

Recently, the idea of curtailing the interest deduction has been on the table for discussion at the congressional level, and nonpartisan organizations are analyzing the potential impacts. Although the deduction will likely survive for the near future, perhaps, with some changes, the days of this subsidy may be numbered.

Canada has learned that interest deduction is not necessary to ensure livable communities and good housing stock. Taxation can be arranged to avoid subsidizing a particular form of tenure. In fact, eliminating the deduction altogether would level the playing field and make lots of different housing types more equal. Even now, some economists have argued that it might make more sense for people to rent rather than own, and to invest money in other ways that ripple through the economy.

Moreover, as pointed out by Roger Lowenstein in the March 5, 2005, *New York Times Magazine* ("Who Needs the Mortgage-Interest Deduction?"), the tax break for home ownership provides neither a significant advantage for the middle class nor encourages ownership, despite our national mythology claiming that it does. In fact, other industrialized countries that do not offer the tax break display similar percentages of home ownership as the U.S. Lowenstein asserts that the tax break primarily serves to encourage wealthier people to buy larger, more expensive houses and even second homes.

FROM COPS ON BIKES TO DOCS ON BIKES: CIRCUIT-RIDING HEALTH CARE

Over the past decade, a number of cities have discovered a more effective way of providing police protection to urban neighborhoods. This is the growing trend of putting cops on bicycles. At first, this seemed naive, almost too passive. But, in fact, it has proven to be both cost-effective and socially effective.

It puts police into communities in a very humane way. It allows for fast, nimble response to emergencies. And it allows police to better serve as "eyes on the street"—or to be more accurate, eyes on the sidewalk, where drug dealing, aggressive panhandling, street crimes, and other antisocial behaviors often occur. It also allows law enforcement professionals to serve other roles: giving directions and information, helping handicapped individuals, referring people to public assistance, reporting broken infrastructure, etc. It puts police in direct contact with citizens.

These same principles could well be applied to other professional services. For example, as baby boomers reach their late 70s and 80s, it may be difficult for them, especially if they have no car, to easily get to doctors. It is possible we could see a return to "house calls" by physicians. This would be immensely practical within downtown areas, where population densities would make short, multiple stops possible.

Doctors and nurses could travel about using bicycles, small motorbikes, or compact, one-seat electric cars—essentially enclosed motorbikes. As small handheld computers become more prevalent, service calls

---

Jump-Starting Downtown Housing Through Tax Incentives

Philadelphia has evidently discovered how to turn on the downtown housing trend full blast. After 40 years of declining population, the Center City is booming with new and rehabilitated housing. Already accommodating the nation's third largest downtown residential population, the Center City's number of households rose by 24 percent between 2000 and 2005. Downtown population increased from 78,000 to 88,000.

The increase is partly a result of a citywide tax abatement program begun in 1997 that originally applied only to residential conversions.

Since 2000, the program has expanded to include new construction and holds the tax assessment at a property's predevelopment level for 10 years.

The Center City District (CCD), a private-sector business improvement district established in 1990, has reported that since the program was passed, an excess of 8,000 converted and new units will have been added to the Center City. The district consists of 120 blocks and more than 2,100 properties. The CCD also reports that 37 percent of downtown residents walk to work, the highest percentage of any American city.

---

could be announced, patient charts could be maintained on the spot, and prescriptions e-mailed immediately. This type of service could be an option offered by health insurance companies for an additional premium.

Alternatively, community centers could include health clinics with rotating staff supplied by larger health care institutions. So much health care is provided by non-physicians today that nurses and medics could perform many functions. Within downtowns, most residential buildings already have short-term load zones and small delivery slots that could be used by circuit-riding medical professionals—a sort of return to the days when doctors put big placards on their cars when they needed to park during an emergency.

THE END OF SOCIAL SECURITY: SHARED AND PART-TIME JOBS

It is becoming increasingly evident that the federal Social Security system will be unable to keep up with the growing demand for benefits as more and more people move into retirement or semiretirement. Even for those receiving private pensions, the income will likely not be sufficient to provide for a decent, comfortable way of life. So people will simply need to work.

The idea of retiring at age 65 will likely disappear, if for no other reason that people are living healthier longer and continue to be able to contribute productively to the economy. Indeed, many people prefer to work—not out of necessity, but simply to remain active and valued.

There is already evidence mounting to suggest this shift of attitude. The 2002 National Study of the Changing Workforce found that many employees are choosing to remain in the workforce during their later years. Employers are adapting to this change as well, since older workers are often more stable and experienced than their younger counterparts.

As reported in that study, figures from the Bureau of Labor Statistics predict that there will be over 26 million workers age 55 and older by the year 2010—approximately 20 percent of the total number of workers in the U.S. Projecting that figure forward a decade might suggest that 26 million people will be retiring once they reach age 65. I believe this is highly unlikely. We will see an entirely new concept of "work" emerge, where people might work fewer than 40 hours per week, but will continue to be actively engaged in work well into their 70s.

This will have enormous implications for employers, who will need to arrange work to allow for part-time positions or allow more people to work from home. Already, technology allows many people to work quite effectively from home locations. With the advent of outsourcing, customers often have no idea where the person they are talking to is actually located. Older workers could provide a good, experienced pool of people who offer assistance by computer or phone.

Moreover, increasing numbers of jobs might be shared, either by two older workers, or, say, a mother working part time and an older worker. Many people are looking for additional sources of income to offset living costs, but desire flexibility due to individual circumstances. The workplace, along with the methods of delivering goods and services, will undergo fundamental and far-reaching transformations over the next few decades.

This new work environment will be vastly easier for older people to manage if they live in a setting where there are multiple opportunities for jobs and services within walking distance. Density actually increases people's freedom by liberating them from a potentially deadening future of isolation and separation from others.

AFTER THE BOX: A BODEGA ON EVERY BLOCK

There is a reason that most big box retail stores are constructed like generic concrete envelopes that could contain almost anything. These businesses know full well that their days are numbered. Well, perhaps not exactly days, but years.

Retailing goes through cycles. The big multistory department stores that grew out of middle-class commerce at the turn of the last century went through their heyday, a period that lasted almost a century. Most of the regional stores have disappeared or have merged with the few remaining national brands. Regional shopping centers reached their peak in the 1990s and now there are hundreds of "dead malls" from coast to coast.

Festival marketplaces came and went even more quickly, as did retail and entertainment centers. The "lifestyle centers"—aggregations of upscale shops and restaurants—currently in vogue will likely have a similarly short-lived cycle. Big box retail and "power centers"—which join together several large national brand stores—may have another good decade, but they too will be transformed, likely by Internet shopping or by a saturation of their own markets.

What we are already beginning to see in many cities is the return of the urban supermarket, a smaller, more compact, and more diverse version of the type found in outlying areas. The hinterlands will likely continue

Fig. 10-4. Small neighborhood groceries, like Ralph's Deli in Seattle's Belltown neighborhood, must be a part of dense urban neighborhoods. Source: Mark Hinshaw.

to see large-footprint, single-story markets surrounded by acres of asphalt. But neighborhoods within and around downtown will not tolerate wasting valuable land for surface parking and sprawling boxes. Some national chains like Target and Costco have developed urban models with structured parking and several floors—ironically, a throwback to the model of the large department stores.

Cities that have witnessed several thousands of new residents during the past decade are seeing the rebirth of small, locally owned, family-operated businesses related to food. These include small food markets, wine stores, cheese shops, artisan bakeries, and places that offer made-to-order meals for take-out or delivery. Many of the new residents of downtown neighborhoods gravitate there precisely because of the wide range of food and drink choices within a short walk.

North American communities have had a long tradition of small-scale entrepreneurial commerce. Many people lament the loss of the mom-and-pop corner store that flourished during the era of large families and low car ownership. Smaller households, car dependency, single-purpose zoning, and low-density development have all combined to effectively make such businesses unprofitable to operate in outlying locations.

Thankfully, we are seeing this form of small-scale capitalism flourish again within dense urban neighborhoods.

FROM ROADWAYS TO *RAMBLAS*

In most American communities streets have been considered principally utilitarian thoroughfares for the movement of vehicles. But a new view has been emerging, that of streets as social spaces. Of course, for some cities this is not a new idea. Many streets in older cities, like Newbury Street in Boston, Fifth Avenue in New York, and Michigan Avenue in Chicago, have for a long time been rich and varied social settings.

In these places, people can enjoy themselves while strolling. They engage in animated conversations—even debates—right on the street corner. They can browse vendors of books, belts, scarves, and other bric-a-brac. They linger over coffee in a sidewalk cafe or simply sit on the steps and watch the passing crowds.

These linear "public living rooms" have existed for hundreds of years in many cities and cultures throughout the world. American cities, however, had a marked paucity of them. Perhaps it is our Puritan roots, a moral belief that idleness was the work of the devil. Perhaps it was a work ethic that gave little time for simple pleasures. Or perhaps it was a tendency to enjoy leisure time in private spaces. Of course, television can also receive a share of the blame, as can the time spent traveling in automobiles for every single need in life.

What is remarkable is that this is changing in cities and towns across the country. For whatever reason, many people are discovering that spending time on public streets is invigorating, sociable, and personally satisfying. In the last decade, entire streets in some urban neighborhoods have small versions of the Italian *passegiata*, with streams of people on foot throughout the day and evening. Sidewalk cafes, open storefronts, small courtyards, awnings, seating, and tiny gardens have sprouted up in numerous communities despite a lack of tradition for such places.

Broadway and Milwaukee's Third Ward

The Historic Third Ward neighborhood is on the National Register of Historic Places as Milwaukee's oldest center of commerce and warehousing. Today it is a showcase mixed use district with retail, new and established family-owned businesses and services, art galleries, theaters, festival grounds, and residential apartments and lofts, most within beautifully restored historic buildings.

Broadway Street has three lively blocks within the historic district. These three blocks contain all of the uses listed above, minus the festival grounds, and more than a few jewels. At one end of this *ramblas* is a new year-round public market, where local farmers sell their produce in indoor and outdoor stalls. Along the first block from the market is Commission Row, which has distributed wholesale groceries and housed commission industries for over 100 years. The family business continues to provide fruit and vegetable produce to the region.

The third block contains the Broadway Theatre Center, which boasts a 385-seat baroque-style theater. There the corridor is neatly capped by Catalano Square, an outdoor park dedicated to Italian families who helped develop the neighborhood at the turn of the 20th century.

Significant public improvement financed by a tax increment district is evident in the Third Ward. In 1992, a $3.4 million streetscapes project was completed, including Catalano Square, two midblock parks on Broadway, scores of pedestrian-scaled light poles, two gateway arches, and more. Parking structures were added in 1994 and 2000, and are owned by the Business Improvement District (BID). These projects were made possible by the efforts of the BID, a nine-member board appointed by the mayor.

Housing units in this energetic neighborhood are steadily increasing. By 2006, there should be over 1,080 units, up from 240 units in 1999.

Streets like N.W. 23rd in Portland, Fifth Avenue in downtown San Diego, Figueroa in downtown Los Angeles, First Avenue in Seattle, and Broadway in Milwaukee's Third Ward all have attributes similar to Spanish *ramblas*. Such streets might be home to some national or even international brands, but they are for the most part chockablock with a host of one-of-kind, locally owned shops, galleries, restaurants, and cafes.

A recent piece in the *New York Times Magazine* ("For Mature Audiences," January 22, 2006) remarked upon "the free-spending, self-inventing boomer generation" and the fact that, unlike the generation that preceded them, they enjoy the social experience of purchasing goods and services. Indeed, their spending power is formidable, amounting to $3 trillion annually. Clearly, this group and people in their 20s are fueling the rapid revitalization of urban centers and urban streets.

Traditionally, Americans have always expressed a preference to live in small towns because of their folksiness and friendliness. Dense neighborhoods act like small towns within a larger city. In a sense, the major walking and shopping streets in and close to downtowns serve as "main streets," allowing people to interact with friends, colleagues, fellow residents, and shopkeepers face-to-face on a daily basis. Accordingly, it is possible to eat one's cake and have it too—access to the commerce and culture of a major city and the intimacy of a small town.

Moreover, the Active Living Network maintains that the health and longevity of people can be greatly enhanced by the simple act of walking to take care of their daily needs. While regular exercise is beneficial, it need not always be in the form of health club regimens. Simply walking throughout the day is healthy. Neighborhoods in and near downtown have a distinct advantage because workplaces, goods and services, and entertainment are all within close proximity. Finally, research by William H. Whyte has shown that people will walk farther when there are interesting things to see and do along the way.

CREATIVE INSTITUTIONS

Large organizations tend not to be open to innovation. They are complex, hierarchical, and slow to respond to change. Governmental units have so many different constituent groups with competing, and even conflicting, demands that it is difficult for agencies to conduct normal business.

But in the coming decades, with their sweeping demographic and economic changes, it will be increasingly necessary for organizations to change both their form and their function. Entirely new methods of delivering products and services will be required. The aging population will alter politics and policy. Populations that choose to live in denser communities will demand services that are currently relegated to outlying locations. As minorities become the majority, they will elect representatives who will simply redirect resources to the needs of their constituents.

Already, there are indications that organizations are rethinking their roles, especially with respect to urban development in general and downtown development in particular. Many transit agencies have moved beyond their core transportation mission to encourage and facilitate a mix of housing and commercial around light rail, commuter rail, and regional bus stations. Some downtown associations have expanded their role in promoting business by taking on issues of social services and affordable housing.

This institutional creativity is not confined to big cities. Smaller communities without entrenched attitudes or actors may be able to adapt more easily. One stunning example is that of Bremerton, Washington, on the west side of Puget Sound.

By the year 2000, downtown Bremerton was all but formally declared dead. Department stores had moved to the suburbs decades before. Storefronts were empty. During the robust years of population growth throughout Puget Sound in the 1990s, Bremerton actually *lost* population.

Norman McLaughlin, executive director of the Kitsap County Consolidated Housing Authority, saw that his agency could play a role in revitalizing downtown Bremerton by stimulating other forms of economic development while continuing to meet affordable housing needs. The city needed a high profile project that would cause people to sit up and take notice. So McLaughlin put together a new government center on a site smack in the middle of downtown to hold a new city hall and a number of county, state, and federal offices. Revenues from lease commitments allowed the authority to issue bonds.

Within a couple of years, Bremerton sported a sparkling new highrise tower. This encouraged the city to move forward with its own project for a conference center, hotel, and town square, which opened not long after the government center. The transit authority pitched in with funding and a commitment to locate its administrative headquarters downtown. Bremerton's new and aggressive mayor, Cary Bozeman, sponsored a number of initiatives to attract private investment, and a new bank and office building were built. And the housing authority has since attracted a major market-rate housing development.

Fig. 10-5. Artist Buster Simpson worked with local architects and landscape architects to design Vine Street in Seattle, which is not only green in the vegetative sense but visibly reflects sustainable building practices of capturing and filtering stormwater runoff. Source: Mark Hinshaw.

In less than five years, downtown Bremerton was transformed from a sad tragedy to a place that is now the envy of other communities. Without the creativity of several institutions, this dramatic change would simply not have happened.

GREEN STREETS, SERENE STREETS

In the last 10 years it has become popular among planners and other professionals to seek to achieve a "24/7" downtown, as if every community should aspire to become small versions of Manhattan, Hong Kong, or Paris. This is, for the most part, highly unlikely in any event, but even so it is wrongheaded. I suspect that most of the people making such declarations do not actually *live* in a downtown.

Says Vancouver city council member Gordon Price, who has been a passionate advocate of density and downtown living: "Let's not try to overshoot, please. An 18-hour downtown is just fine, thank you. Most human beings need to get at least six hours of sleep. At least I know I do."

Perhaps planners have been overly zealous in taking to heart the late Jane Jacobs's call to appreciate density and diversity. But even Jacobs's beloved Greenwich Village is not universally busy day and night. There are quiet, tree-lined streets with row houses whose bedroom windows overlook the sidewalk.

Even midtown Manhattan, with some of the highest densities in the world, has streets that are relatively unbusy, serene, and residential in character. In fact, as one walks into one of those long side streets, the noise level from the big avenue immediately dies down and the sights and scents of vegetation are apparent. Even normal, quiet conversation is possible.

Manhattan had a long-standing zoning concept that placed commercial uses and tall buildings on the avenues and mid-rise residential uses on the side streets. This worked for many years, offering the choice of either hustle and bustle or quietude. Vancouver borrowed this idea in much of its central city zoning. Dense but purely residential districts of four to eight blocks in width are separated by commercial streets that offer every form of shopping, food, and entertainment imaginable. Residents live in quiet places but can walk only five minutes to bustling streets for anything they need. This pattern of urban development is sometimes called "horizontal mixed use."

We will need to craft tools like this for our downtowns. Too often, we have developed crude regulations that are, in a sense, "one size" to fit all conditions. Rather than such a blunt instrument, we need approaches that are more akin to surgical precision if we are to ensure that downtowns are truly livable.

TAILORING TRANSIT

As the baby boom generation ages, many people will begin to realize that they will no longer be able to depend upon their own car for transportation. If the state where they reside doesn't decline to renew their license, their insurance company will likely raise its rates significantly. Insurance companies will certainly use traffic accident data to raise premiums.

One way or another, many millions of people will need to have other means available to get around. Already, of course, services like "dial-a-ride" buses and special vans for handicapped individuals are becoming widely available in cities. But other forms of transportation will need to be developed.

A number of cities have begun to bring back an old form of transit: the streetcar. This form of public transit is, of course, fixed, so that private investment can respond to the permanence of the alignment. But it also allows residents to be able to depend upon regular service.

Streetcars travel in the roadbed, so no costly right-of-way is necessary. They operate at relatively slow speeds, so they are compatible with other vehicles and pedestrians. They can make stops every few blocks, often without any special station facility other than, perhaps, a handicapped ramp. They also stimulate corridors and nodes of shops and services. The streetcar is ideal for dense urban neighborhoods, as it is quiet and nonpolluting. So, we will likely see the return of the streetcar—ironically, a form of transport that served cities well 100 years ago.

Rails might not even be needed. There are a number of cities that have electric trolley buses, a form of transportation that has many of the advantages of the streetcar on tracks. They are quiet and pollution-free.

But despite the higher capital cost, there is nothing that seems to substitute for the pure pleasure of riding in a train. Though it may be purely visceral and psychological, most people hold trains in higher esteem than buses, no matter how clean or dependable they may be.

Over the next several decades, other forms of transport could emerge. Even now some cities have private companies that offer a motorized or human-powered tricycle with two seats for passengers. These are frequently found in tourist areas. But it's not a difficult stretch to imagine a fleet of them, each mounted with a small fare box or meter. I have no doubt that some enterprising young company is planning just such a service, perhaps with enclosed cabs.

Very compact, three-wheeled electric-powered vehicles are already available only for use on local, lower speed local streets. These have bubble-shaped acrylic envelopes that surround a single seat. States might issue a differentiated license that allows older people to operate such vehicles within a prescribed neighborhood area.

Finally, increasingly sophisticated scooters are being produced for people with physical impairments. These operate on sidewalks and are compatible with walking speeds. This type of vehicle could be produced not just for people with severe impairments, but for those with more modest limitations. Imagine this type of vehicle with a couple of seats mounted on it. Of course, this is not far from what some people now use for golfing and, indeed, some retirement communities allow the use of such vehicles on their own internal lanes. But with improved technology, whole new types of vehicles—both for single and multiple occupants—will likely emerge.

Hispanic Neighborhoods in Chicago

Chicago not only has a large Hispanic population—about 26 percent of the city's residents—the population itself is also diverse, with Mexican Americans, Puerto Ricans, and people from many South American countries. Over time many of these people have been displaced as their neighborhoods have become gentrified. Grassroots efforts in the last few years have led to public programs to educate Spanish-speaking (as well as other language-speaking) home owners on property tax exemptions and other tools.

Meanwhile, one Puerto Rican neighborhood and one Mexican American neighborhood have managed to profit from their cultural assets without resorting to gentrification. In the Humboldt Park neighborhood, a six-block stretch of Division Street is nicknamed *Paseo Boricua*, or Puerto Rican Avenue. The corridor has restaurants, an arts venue for poetry slams and music events, a Puerto Rican cultural center, and other ethnic businesses.

However, the popularity of a district brings new development. Unless specific measures are taken, the very diversity that attracts people to the neighborhood can disappear. For this reason, the Division Street Business Development Association considers affordable housing a priority.

The Pilsen neighborhood represents the center of Chicago's Mexican American community, with the Mexican Fine Arts Center Museum serving as the cultural anchor and economic catalyst. When a large and popular Mexican art exhibit was shown, the museum put together a marketing effort to guide tourists all over the neighborhood and to area restaurants. It also helped develop a trolley system that connects Pilsen with Chinatown in order to encourage even more visitors. Local merchants and national brand sponsors pay for the cost of the trolley, which underscores the principle that cultural tourism should be in the hands of people from the neighborhood.

SSL: SPANISH AS A SECOND LANGUAGE

If the United States ever was a melting pot, as high school textbooks used to say, it certainly is not now. Increasingly we are a pluralistic culture with many different peoples living side by side. Each group has its own heritage, traditions, language, and values. This diverse mix of cultures is found most often in central cities. We are a polyglot country as never before. In many larger cities, more than 100 languages and dialects are spoken. Major airports now must make announcements in more than one tongue. Cash machines already offer choices of language in many places.

Just as European countries have seen English terms creep into their everyday vocabulary, we in this country have incorporated words from Spanish, French, Japanese, Russian, and Middle Eastern languages. Around many major cities, inner-ring suburban areas are being filled with immigrants from around the world, much like earlier Italian and Jewish families settled into outer areas of New York 100 years ago. It is not uncommon to find a Korean grocery, a Thai restaurant, or even a Ukrainian bakery in almost any part of any city.

As the white population declines, we are shifting toward a culture in which no ethnic group will predominate. By the year 2050, there will only be minority groups making up the population.

While in general family sizes are getting smaller across the board, there is one exception: Hispanic households. Now it is possible to speculate that even this group will see a decline in family size as education and income levels increase (as has occurred with other ethnic groups). Even so, the 2000 census marked an important turning point: For the first time, Hispanics and Latinos outnumbered African Americans as the largest nonwhite minority. It is certainly likely that Hispanics will play a much larger role in politics, the economy, and popular culture.

Already, several states such as California, Arizona, Texas, and Florida have seen this trend. But Hispanics are now found in significant numbers throughout the country, not just in the states closest to Central America. At some point in the next several decades, people whose main language is English may need to enroll in SSL (Spanish as a Second Language) classes just to be able to be able to fully understand the nuances of changing commerce and entertainment. Signs of this language shift are already apparent. A construction site near where I live has a big placard posted for workers. The Spanish text is printed with the words larger than those in English.

TIME-SHARE CARS

In the past several years in a number of cities, the idea of sharing vehicles has become popular. At least two companies, Flexcar and Zipcar, offer people an option to subscribe to a program where vehicles can be checked out or reserved in advance for a monthly fee. A variety of cars and trucks are offered, so that people can have many choices readily available depending on the need. Reservations can be made online and multiple pickup locations are typically available. Many of the vehicles are hybrids with high fuel efficiency.

The density found in and near downtowns makes this program especially cost-effective. It also allows downtown residents to avoid having a car altogether. As fuel and insurance costs inevitably increase, this new way of having access to vehicles will likely increase in popularity.

Fig. 10-6. The last image in this book about urban living is of a car—but a car with a twist. Flexcar offers vehicles that are shared by dozens of households, a trend that may well become more widespread as petroleum gets more costly. Source: Mark Hinshaw.

Epilogue

So here we are, well into the first decade of the 21st century. Already it is evident that we are surrounded by dramatically changing demographics, a different economy, and many new and emerging social imperatives. It is clear that many people are rediscovering city centers, not just as concentrations of commerce and culture but as places to live.

After decades of decline, downtowns are coming back, perhaps with a vengeance. And it might also be that the very notion of what constitutes downtowns is changing. Most of the downtowns we have examined have acquired, over the last six or seven years, a ring of dense urban neighborhoods in areas that previously were only underused commercial or industrial buildings or parking lots. Often these districts, while closely associated with their cores, have their own distinct names. In many cities, this phenomenon is so recent that the 2000 census did not catch it.

Americans have always had ambivalent attitudes towards downtowns. We have recognized urban centers for their roles in business, specialized medicine, education, arts, and major league sports, but we have not seen them as being livable. At the same time, we have long professed a love for small towns, with their sociability and intimacy. Now, many people are realizing that they can have both—access to many different choices *and* a sense of neighborliness.

Remarkably, this new attitude toward downtowns is being seen in many places across the United States, not just in big cities but also in inner-ring suburbs that are transforming into cities and even in mid-sized, freestanding towns. The rapidity with which this is occurring is almost breathtaking.

In some ways, we have simply rediscovered our roots. Many of our original notions of democracy, social services, artistic endeavors, and civic life came from people who lived in the cities of our colonial and newly independent eras. Back then, denser communities offered many of the attributes that we continue to look for in places to live. Perhaps the second half of the 20th century was merely a dark period from which we are finally emerging.

This renewed enthusiasm for city centers holds a heartening promise for the next 50 years. We are building communities that once again embody the convenience, choice, and richness that density and diversity offer.

Selected Bibliography

Alexander, Christopher and Murray Silverstein, et al. 1977. *A Pattern Language*. New York: Oxford University Press.

Appleyard, Donald. *Livable Streets*. 1981. Berkeley: University of California Press.

Barnett, Jonathan. 1996. *The Fractured Metropolis: Improving the New City, Restoring the Old City, Reshaping the Region*. New York: HarperCollins.

Beatley, Timothy. 2000. *Green Urbanism: Learning from European Cities*. Washington, D.C.: Island Press.

Birch, Eugenie L. November 2005. "Who Lives Downtown?" The Brookings Institution.

Birch, Eugenie L. May 2005. "Who Lives Downtown Today (And Are They Any Different from Downtowners of Thirty Years Ago?)" Boston: Lincoln Institute of Land Policy.

Breen, Ann and Dick Rigby. 2004. *Intown Living: A Different American Dream*. Washington, D.C.: Island Press.

Callenbach, Ernest. 1975. *Ecotopia*: New York: Bantam.

Calthorpe, Peter. 1993. *The Next American Metropolis: Ecology, Community and the American Dream*. Princeton, N.J.: Princeton Architectural Press.

Cervero, Robert. 1998. *The Transit Metropolis: A Global Inquiry*. Washington, D.C.: Island Press.

Engwicht, David. 1993. *Reclaiming Our Cities and Towns: Better Living with Less Traffic*. Philadelphia: New Society Publishers.

Ford, Larry. 1994. *Cities and Buildings*. Baltimore: Johns Hopkins University Press.

Fulton, William and Peter Calthorpe. 2001. *The Regional City: Planning for the End of Sprawl*. Washington, D.C.: Island Press.

Garvin, Alexander. 1996. *The American City*. New York: McGraw-Hill.

Hall, Peter Geoffrey. 1996. *Cities of Tomorrow: Planning and Design in the Twentieth Century*. Oxford, U.K.: Blackwell Publishing.

Hayden, Dolores. 1984. *Redesigning the American Dream: The Future of Housing, Work and Family Life*. New York: W. W. Norton & Company.

Hayden, Dolores. 2004. *A Field Guide to Sprawl*. New York: W. W. Norton & Company.

Hiss, Tony. 1990. *The Experience of Place: A New Way of Looking At and Dealing with Our Radically Changing Cities and Countryside*. New York: Random House.

Jackson, Kenneth T. 1987. *Crabgrass Frontier: The Suburbanization of the United States*. New York: Oxford University Press.

Jacobs, Allan. *Great Streets*. Cambridge, Mass.: MIT Press, 1993.

Jacobs, Allan. *Making City Planning Work*. American Society of Planning Officials, 1978.

Jacobs, Jane. 1961. *The Death and Life of Great American Cities*. New York: Vintage Books.

Jacobs, Jane. 1969. *The Economy of Cities*. New York: Random House.

Keeney, Gavin, John Hunt Dixon, and Allen S. Weiss. 2001. *On the Nature of Things*. Birkhauser.

Kostof, Spiro. 1991. *The City Shaped: Urban Patterns and Meanings Through History*. Boston: Bulfinch.

Kuntsler, James Howard. 1993. *The Geography of Nowhere: The Rise and Decline of America's Man-Made Landscape*. New York: Simon and Schuster.

Lynch, Kevin. 1981. *A Theory of Good City Form*. Cambridge, Mass.: MIT Press.

Lynch, Kevin. 1960. *The Image of the City*. Cambridge, Mass.: MIT Press.

McHarg, Ian. 1969. *Design with Nature*. New York: Doubleday Natural History Press.

Mollenkopf, John H. 1983. *The Contested City*. Princeton, N.J.: Princeton University Press.

Moore, Terry and Paul Thorsnes. 1994. *The Transportation/Land Use Connection*. American Planning Association Planning Advisory Service Report 448/449.

Moudon, Anne Vernez, ed. 1987. *Public Streets for Public Use*. New York: Columbia University Press.

Newman, Oscar. 1972. *Defensible Space: Crime Prevention Through Urban Design*. New York: MacMillan Company.

Newman, P. and J. Kenworthy. 1989. *Cities and Automobile Dependence*. Aldershot, U.K.: Gower Publishing.

Oldenberg, Ray, 1991. *The Great Good Place*. New York: Paragon House.

Peirce, Neal. 1993. *Citistates: How Urban America Can Prosper in a Competitive World*. Washington, D.C.: Seven Locks Press.

Putnam, Robert. 2000. *Bowling Alone: The Collapse and Revival of the American Community*, New York: Simon and Schuster.

Rothblatt, Donald N. and Andrew Sancton. 1993. *Metropolitan Governance: American/Canadian Intergovernmental Perspectives*. Berkeley: University of California Press.

Sennett, Richard. 1970. *The Uses of Disorder*. New York: Alfred Knopf.

Sucher, David. 2003. *City Comforts*. (self-published)

Vance, James. 1990. *The Continuing City: Urban Morphology and Western Civilization*. Baltimore: Johns Hopkins University Press.

Vuchic, Vukan R. 1999. *Transportation for Livable Cities*. New Brunswick, N.J.: CUPR Press.

Whyte, William H. 1998. *City: Rediscovering the Center*. New York: The Conservation Foundation.

Wirth, Louis. "Urbanism as a Way of Life," in *American Journal of Sociology*, 44 (1938) 1–24.

Appendix:
Selected Case Studies

DESCRIPTIONS AND DATA OF SELECTED DOWNTOWNS

Graphics and Information created and compiled by Sarah M. Durkee

INTRODUCTION

The downtowns described in this appendix are not intended to be an exhaustive listing of places where downtown living is increasingly prevalent, but rather a representative selection. Much of the data was derived from a research study conducted by University of Pennsylvania Professor Eugenie Birch for the Lincoln Institute of Land Policy. Birch's analysis focused on 44 cities, some of which have not seen the phenomenon of downtown living. Moreover, the cities highlighted in the report were also selective and did not include some cities, such as San Jose, California, which have also seen similar change. Nor did it include rapidly transforming suburbs, such as Bethesda, Maryland; Bellevue, Washington; or Glendale, California, which are also seeing significant numbers of new, dense urban housing developments.

Furthermore, the census data Birch relied upon only carried the research to the year 2000, the most recent census year. Many downtowns, such as San Diego's, have seen major increases in downtown population since that year. We have attempted to predict the continuing change during this decade by inquiring with agencies and organizations that monitor construction and building permits in each city, so that there is some confidence that the population forecast will be reflected by actual occupied dwelling units and not mere speculation.

In the course of talking with agencies and organizations in various cities, it became evident that the entire notion of "downtown" is going through a transformation. Some cities are now referring to a "center city," which embraces adjacent districts occupied by industry or parking lots only a few years ago. In some cities it is these areas that have seen the greatest amount of change with respect to residential development. For example, Atlanta's Castleberry District, just to the south of the older commercial core, had been filled with warehouses and fabricators but is now largely loft conversions. In Portland, the River District—now renamed the Pearl District—has become a concentration of mid-rise and high-rise housing, largely in the last six years.

It is entirely clear that, despite any geographic redefinition of downtown, the trend towards urban residential development in city centers is robust and, in some places, quite dramatic.

COMPARATIVE STUDY OF DOWNTOWN POPULATIONS

Downtown Population Over 10,000 People

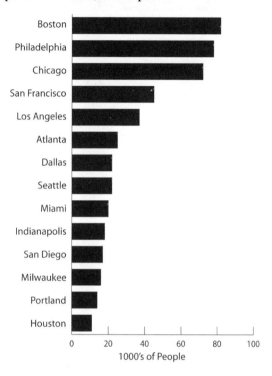

Source: "Who Lives Downtown Today (And Are They Any Different from Downtowners of Thirty Years Ago)?" prepared for the Lincoln Institute of Land Planning by Eugenie L. Birch, May 2005

Downtown Densities in Downtowns Greater Than 7,000 People per Mile

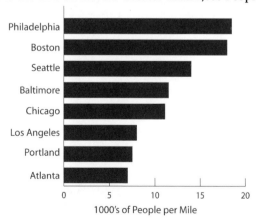

Source: Fannie May Foundation, Rebecca R. Sohmer and Robert E. Lang, May 2001

Increase in Downtown Populations 1990–2000

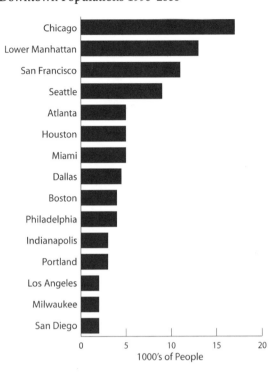

Source: "Who Lives Downtown Today (And Are They Any Different from Downtowners of Thirty Years Ago)?" prepared for the Lincoln Institute of Land Planning by Eugenie L. Birch, May 2005

Percent Increase in Downtown Populations 1990–2000

Source: "Who Lives Downtown Today (And Are They Any Different from Downtowners of Thirty Years Ago)?" prepared for the Lincoln Institute of Land Planning by Eugenie L. Birch, May 2005

ATLANTA

Atlanta Downtown Area

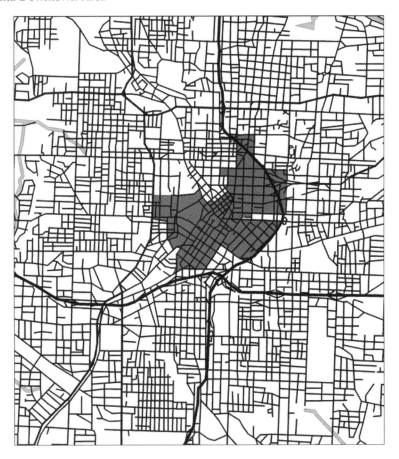

1/2 inch = 1 mile. Source: Copyright 2002 ESRI; used with permission

Atlanta's downtown is approximately two miles in the east/west direction and two miles in the north/south direction. Jennifer Ball, with Central Atlanta Progress, which shepherds downtown development, attributes the growing livability of downtown to four key actions: the use of Tax Allocation Districts (aka Tax Increment Financing) to provide incentives for housing; the Atlanta Downtown Improvement District, which improved safety and cleanliness; the Atlanta Regional Commission and its Livable Centers initiative, which coordinated planning for mixed use centers with transportation; and finally, the 1996 Olympic Games, which caused the improvement of parks and infrastructure.

CAP also sponsored educational forums for developers and brokers, as well as tours of downtown housing aimed at consumers. As a result, new housing has been built in many parts of downtown, including conversions of older office buildings, in the artsy Castleberry Warehouse district and near Olympic Park.

In addition to the older downtown commercial core, there is a newer and rapidly burgeoning area known as Midtown, just north of the downtown. This district is being dramatically transformed by dense, mid- and high-rise residential buildings.

According to Catherine Fox, the arts and architecture writer for the *Atlanta Journal-Constitution*, the Midtown area benefited from a plan that has been largely followed. Initial investments in cultural venues such as the expansive High Museum have infused the area with a definite cachet. Stylish structures—some traditionally sedate, others more exuberantly contemporary—rise up from an understory of quaint older structures, some dating back more than 100 years. These are frequently occupied by specialty stores, galleries, and a slew of ethnic restaurants.

In contrast to the downtown core, which is marked by sky bridges and bunker-like hotels and shopping malls, Midtown has a vibrant street life with sidewalk cafes, street trees, public spaces, and a wide variety of commercial and cultural choices. The large and stately Piedmont Park gives the district an "old world" feel, despite the insertions of dense modern buildings. The area even has acquired its own distinctive skyline with fancifully topped buildings, some outfitted with dramatic lighting.

According to Central Atlanta Progress, more than 3,800 units of housing have been built within and near downtown since the year 2000. Another 7,000 are under construction and more are planned.

Atlanta Downtown Resident Data

Income	Median Low: $8,469
	Median High: $40,906
Race and Ethnicity	White: 19.2%
	Black: 75.7%
	Asian: 1.3%
	Hispanic: 4.0%
Age	Under 18: 18%
	18-24: 23%
	25-34: 20%
	35-44: 16%
	45-64: 16%
	Over 65: 8%
Educational Attainment	H.S. Diploma: 33%
	Bachelor Degree: 24%
	Graduate Degree: 9%

Information for 2000. Source: "Who Lives Downtown Today (And Are They Any Different from Downtowners of Thirty Years Ago)?" prepared for the Lincoln Institute of Land Planning by Eugenie L. Birch, May 2005

Atlanta Downtown Population

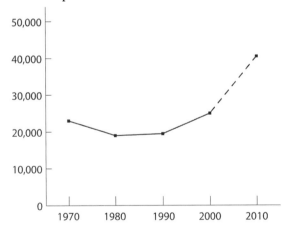

1. Numbers for 1970, 1980, 1990, and 2000 are taken from "Who Lives Downtown Today (And Are They Any Different from Downtowners of Thirty Years Ago)?" prepared for the Lincoln Institute of Land Planning by Eugenie L. Birch, May 2005.
2. Number for 2010 estimated as a result of data from agencies in each city.

BOSTON

Boston Downtown Area

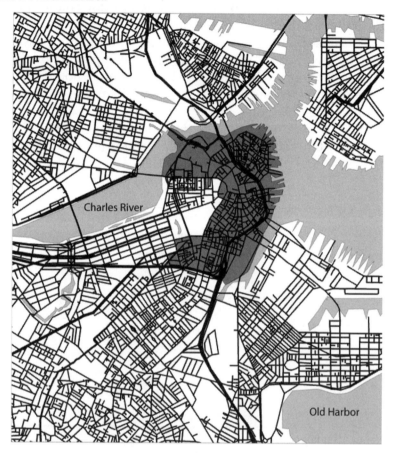

1/2 inch = 1 mile. Source: Copyright 2002 ESRI; used with permission

Boston has had a long tradition of dense neighborhoods close to the downtown core. Housing in the Back Bay and near the Common has continued to be solid and livable, supporting lively streets like Newbury. The North End has been a mainstay of ethnic populations used to living above shops and restaurants. If anything, Boston lost some of its tradition during the era of urban renewal, when whole areas were gutted.

But even so, people are rediscovering downtown as a place to live. This has been assisted by the preservation of a large stock of historic buildings, some of which have been converted to lofts and condominiums. Since the 1980s the city has promoted mixed use development through its Redevelopment Authority (BRA). A number of elegant public spaces has been provided throughout the core.

Rebecca Barnes, the city's former planning director, credits the cleanup of the harbor with attracting new development, including dense residential. Massachusetts has also provided financing to ensure the provision of low-income housing. Recently, completion of the "Big Dig," with its landscaped lid, promises to attract more housing along its edges, as the formerly elevated freeway with its noise, pollution, and visual intrusion is now gone.

According to John Avault of the Boston Redevelopment Authority, downtown Boston should expect to see 4,000 units built during this decade.

Boston Downtown Resident Data

Income	Median Low: $12,165
	Median High: $81,804
Race and Ethnicity	White: 75.3%
	Black: 5.0%
	Asian: 14.3%
	Hispanic: 7.4%
Age	Under 18: 8%
	18-24: 20%
	25-34: 29%
	35-44: 14%
	45-64: 18%
	Over 65: 11%
Educational Attainment	H.S. Diploma: 13%
	Bachelor Degree: 64%
	Graduate Degree: 31%

Information for 2000. Source: "Who Lives Downtown Today (And Are They Any Different from Downtowners of Thirty Years Ago)?" prepared for the Lincoln Institute of Land Planning by Eugenie L. Birch, May 2005

Boston Downtown Population

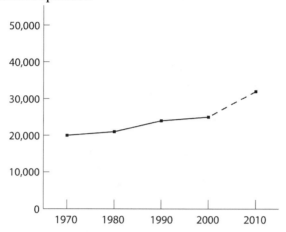

Data provided by John Avault with the Boston Redevelopment Authority. Population is for Boston's Central District, which does not include adjacent urban neighborhoods such as Back Bay.

CHICAGO

Chicago Downtown Area

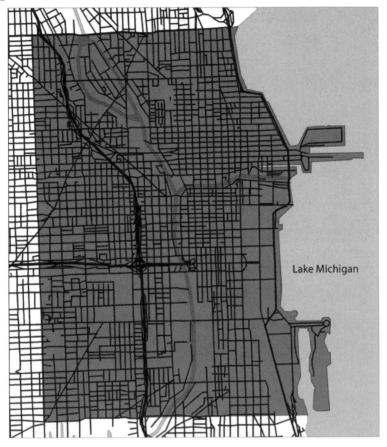

Lake Michigan

1/2 inch = 1 mile. Source: Copyright 2002 ESRI; used with permission

For many decades, downtown Chicago was flanked by robust urban neighborhoods, filled with a mix of industries and working-class homes. As the commercial core expanded outward, factories and warehouses were closed or replaced with parking lots. In the 1960s urban renewal claimed many areas. The result was a very fragmented pattern of uses with large expanses of asphalt—areas that are now seeing significant and dense infill development, ranging from mid-rise to high-rise housing.

The River North district in particular has been dramatically transformed with new housing developments, but housing has also been added to the Loop, the traditional commercial core, and to the areas east of Michigan Avenue north of the river. The reopening of the State Street pedestrian mall to traffic, followed by an aggressive emphasis on visual and performing arts, and a bold new plan for cultural venues in Millennium Park, have stimulated much new interest in downtown as an exciting and appealing place to live.

According to Ron Thomas, executive director of the Northeastern Illinois Planning Commission, credit goes to Mayor Richard M. Daley for initiatives to clean up, fix up, and promote downtown. As many know, the city's "ward" politics have always been Byzantine at best, but Daley has managed to direct coordinated efforts by major public agencies, including the CTA, the Chicago Transit Authority. His leadership has been matched by other elected leaders and by a number of astute developers who have raised the bar of expectation for downtown development.

According to Marie Bousfield of the Chicago Planning and Development Department, more than 19,000 housing units have been built in downtown since 2000. Eighteen thousand more are under construction or in the permitting process.

Chicago Downtown Resident Data

Income	Median Low: $4,602
	Median High: $97,940
Race and Ethnicity	White: 69.3%
	Black: 18.7%
	Asian: 8.5%
	Hispanic: 4.6%
Age	Under 18: 9%
	18-24: 11%
	25-34: 29%
	35-44: 18%
	45-64: 23%
	Over 65: 10%
Educational Attainment	H.S. Diploma: 6%
	Bachelor Degree: 68%
	Graduate Degree: 33%

Information for 2000. Source: "Who Lives Downtown Today (And Are They Any Different from Downtowners of Thirty Years Ago)?" prepared for the Lincoln Institute of Land Planning by Eugenie L. Birch, May 2005

Chicago Downtown Population

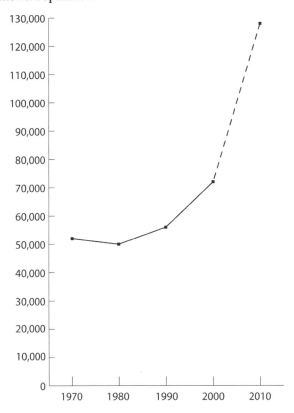

1. *Numbers for 1970, 1980, 1990, and 2000 are taken from "Who Lives Downtown Today (And Are They Any Different from Downtowners of Thirty Years Ago)?" prepared for the Lincoln Institute of Land Planning by Eugenie L. Birch, May 2005.*
2. *Number for 2010 estimated as a result of data from agencies in each city.*

CLEVELAND

Cleveland Downtown Area

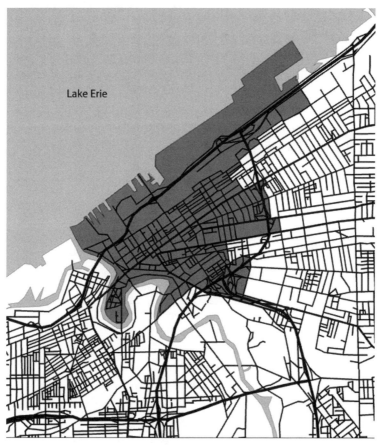

1/2 inch = 1 mile. Source: Copyright 2002 ESRI; used with permission

Cleveland is a classic example of a Midwestern industrial city that lost its blue collar job base and consequently, a good chunk of its population. With the shrinkage, the downtown core—once large, dense, and robust—has struggled for a couple of decades. Block after block of solid, but abandoned, brick commercial buildings line streets like Euclid Avenue.

However, in the last decade, the city has enticed urban dwellers back into downtown by offering tax advantages in return for the conversion of older commercial buildings into housing. This has been both in the form of outright property tax abatements (for 10 years) and a liberal use of tax credits for renovation of structures designated as historic.

Two downtown neighborhoods, the Historic Gateway and the Warehouse District, have seen thousands of units produced through conversion, mostly in the form of rental apartments. According to Tom Yablonsky of the Department of Neighborhoods, downtown now has almost 10,000 new residents. Many of these residents are attracted to the appeal not only of living in charming older buildings, but also of having access to unique restaurants, theaters, museums, blues clubs, and the proximity to an expansive downtown retail center with numerous upscale shops and movie theaters, developed by Cleveland-based Forest City Development Co. The downtown now has sufficient population to attract a locally owned, full-service supermarket.

Cleveland Downtown Resident Data

Income	Median Low: $6,336
	Median High: $50,568
Race and Ethnicity	White: 28.9%
	Black: 63.2%
	Asian: 4.1%
	Hispanic: 3.2%
Age	Under 18: 17%
	18-24: 22%
	25-34: 24%
	35-44: 16%
	45-64: 16%
	Over 65: 7%
Educational Attainment	H.S. Diploma: 21%
	Bachelor Degree: 27%
	Graduate Degree: 11%

Information for 2000. Source: "Who Lives Downtown Today (And Are They Any Different from Downtowners of Thirty Years Ago)?" prepared for the Lincoln Institute of Land Planning by Eugenie L. Birch, May 2005

Cleveland Downtown Population

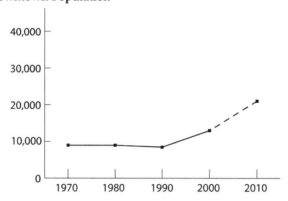

1. *Numbers for 1970, 1980, 1990, and 2000 are taken from "Who Lives Downtown Today (And Are They Any Different from Downtowners of Thirty Years Ago)?" prepared for the Lincoln Institute of Land Planning by Eugenie L. Birch, May 2005.*
2. *Number for 2010 estimated as a result of data from agencies in each city.*

DENVER

Denver Downtown Area

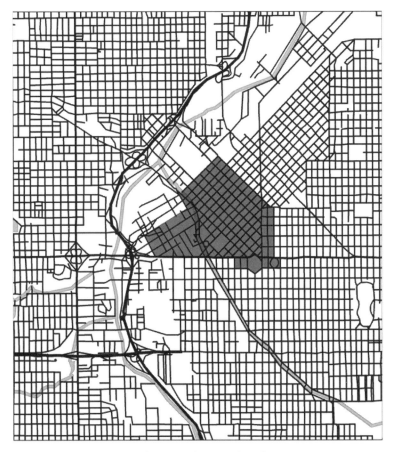

1/2 inch – 1 mile. Source: Copyright 2002 ESRI; used with permission

For many years the Denver metropolitan area was characterized by outward growth spreading into distant suburbs and exurbs. Downtown contained some interesting districts with historic buildings, but these were eclipsed by enormous office buildings for energy companies. The core was almost entirely composed of office towers, hotels, and restaurants aimed at visitors. Outside of a handful of active pockets, even retail struggled. Many parts of downtown were dominated by immense parking structures or open parking lots.

In the 1990s, Denver began to encourage the conversion of old warehouses in the Lower Downtown historic district into offices, lofts, apartments, and live/work spaces. The streetscape was enhanced and art galleries and design firms began to move in. The addition of Coors Field provided a solid anchor, as did the rehabilitation of the grand old Union Station. Lower Downtown continues to be an attractive place to live.

But on the south side, near the Civic Center, a whole new neighborhood has begun to emerge. Called the Golden Triangle, it is a lively mix of older structures, including a magnificently restored school, low- and mid-rise apartments and lofts, and a number of high-rise residential buildings. Part of this new district's cachet comes from being adjacent to the new art museum, with its bold, crystalline forms and the quirky new public library, built a decade ago. The State Capitol building, with its gold-tipped dome, is also a few blocks away. The Golden Triangle is a somewhat messy melange of old and new, funky and elegant, stately and odd. But it is clearly vibrant and sought after as a place to live.

Marilee Utter, formerly the city's director of asset management and now an economic development consultant, credits much of the turnaround to the Denver Partnership, an organization that facilitated investment in infrastructure and attractions, as well as attracting private parties to build in downtown. She also attributes the success of downtown living to a number of specific public sector actions. First came the creation of the Lower Downtown Historic District, which gave it stability and a cachet. The building of Commons Park was also a key investment, as was the new downtown library and the Black History Museum. The city also reduced parking requirements for development near transit stations and converted a major one-way street to a more pedestrian-friendly two-way. She also notes the extensive use of low-income tax credits for the development of workforce housing.

According to the Denver Partnership, which tracks development in the city, since 2000, 7,000 new dwelling units have come on line, with another 1,600 being built. Another 4,000 are in the permit or planning stages.

Denver Downtown Resident Data

Income	Median Low: $30,607
	Median High: $33,750
Race and Ethnicity	White: 80.3%
	Black: 5.5%
	Asian: 6.5%
	Hispanic: 10.5%
Age	Under 18: 2%
	18-24: 8%
	25-34: 24%
	35-44: 16%
	45-64: 21%
	Over 65: 15%
Educational Attainment	H.S. Diploma: 18%
	Bachelor Degree: 48%
	Graduate Degree: 18%

Information for 2000. Source: "Who Lives Downtown Today (And Are They Any Different from Downtowners of Thirty Years Ago)?" prepared for the Lincoln Institute of Land Planning by Eugenie L. Birch, May 2005

Denver Downtown Population

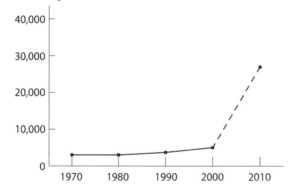

1. Numbers for 1970, 1980, 1990, and 2000 are taken from "Who Lives Downtown Today (And Are They Any Different from Downtowners of Thirty Years Ago)?" prepared for the Lincoln Institute of Land Planning by Eugenie L. Birch, May 2005.
2. Number for 2010 estimated as a result of data from agencies in each city.

HOUSTON

Houston Downtown Area

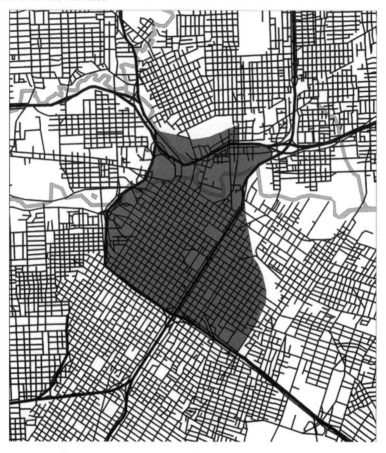

1/2 inch = 1 mile. Source: Copyright 2002 ESRI; used with permission

For several decades, downtown Houston contained only a few thousand residents. But in the decade leading up to 2000, this changed dramatically. Of all downtowns in the U.S., Houston's population experienced one of the most sizable increases with respect to percent increase.

Bob Litke served as planning director between 1991 and 2005. He says Houston took a number of actions during that period to encourage residential development downtown. First, standards and procedures were simplified. Some standards, such as setbacks along certain streets, were eliminated altogether. Tax incentives were enacted to stimulate the preservation of historic buildings and to convert them to residential use. The conversion of the old, decrepit, but originally elegant Rice Hotel served as a stunning example of what could be done.

Downtown Houston also formed a Business Improvement District (BID) that promoted facade renovations and created an environment in which investors would be welcome. The city also expanded its Tax Increment Financing district to include the downtown. This funding source was used to pay back developers for making improvements to streets, sidewalks, and utilities. As a result, not only did downtown see significant changes, but adjacent districts, such as Midtown and the 4th Ward, have also seen major increases in housing.

According to Bob Yuri of the Central Houston Association, several thousand more downtown residents are expected during this decade.

Houston Downtown Resident Data

Income	Median Low: * Median High: *
Race and Ethnicity	White: 56.7% Black: 40.9% Asian: 1.1% Hispanic: 22.6%
Age	Under 18: 4% 18-24: 25% 25-34: 29% 35-44: 25% 45-64: 14% Over 65: 3%
Educational Attainment	H.S. Diploma: 29.4% Bachelor Degree: 4.4% Graduate Degree: 5.1%

* *No information given. Information for 2000.* Source: "Who Lives Downtown Today (And Are They Any Different from Downtowners of Thirty Years Ago)?" prepared for the Lincoln Institute of Land Planning by Eugenie L. Birch, May 2005

Houston Downtown Population

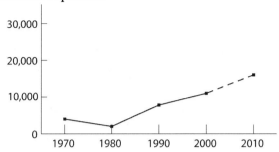

1. Numbers for 1970, 1980, 1990, and 2000 are taken from "Who Lives Downtown Today (And Are They Any Different from Downtowners of Thirty Years Ago)?" prepared for the Lincoln Institute of Land Planning by Eugenie L. Birch, May 2005.
2. Number for 2010 estimated as a result of data from agencies in each city.

INDIANAPOLIS

Indianapolis Downtown Area

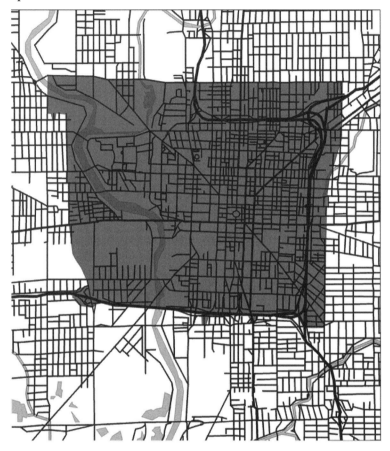

1/2 inch = 1 mile. Source: Copyright 2002 ESRI; used with permission

William Hudnut served as mayor of this city for 16 years, between 1976 and 1991. During his tenure, many key investments were made within the downtown area that are now bearing fruit with respect to attracting residential and mixed use development. New residents enjoy proximity to shops, services, and entertainment.

Hudnut's passionate advocacy of downtown development was carried out through a series of actions. Tax credits for rehabbing historic buildings produced new downtown housing. His administration worked with a developer to turn its Industrial Canal into a common flanked by dense housing. A failed public housing project, Lockfield Gardens, was demolished and replaced with a livable urban neighborhood of mixed income housing adjacent to the Indiana University hospital. Several major attractions were built, including sports stadiums, a convention center, and a retail/entertainment complex. Hudnut also worked to retain corporations downtown, some of which were about to flee to the suburbs. He also commissioned a market study that showed a demand for 5,000 units of housing downtown—a projection that has been exceeded. Hudnut credits the current mayor with adding an emphasis on the arts, which continues to attract more residents.

According to Indianapolis Downtown Inc., 2,000 units of housing have been built since 2000. Another 1,800 units will be completed by 2010.

Indianapolis Downtown Resident Data

Income	Median Low: $12,154
	Median High: $33,650
Race and Ethnicity	White: 58.0%
	Black: 35.0%
	Asian: 2.3%
	Hispanic: 5.9%
Age	Under 18: 12%
	18-24: 18%
	25-34: 25%
	35-44: 18%
	45-64: 18%
	Over 65: 9%
Educational Attainment	H.S. Diploma: 29%
	Bachelor Degree: 24%
	Graduate Degree: 10%

Information for 2000. Source: "Who Lives Downtown Today (And Are They Any Different from Downtowners of Thirty Years Ago)?" prepared for the Lincoln Institute of Land Planning by Eugenie L. Birch, May 2005

Indianapolis Downtown Population

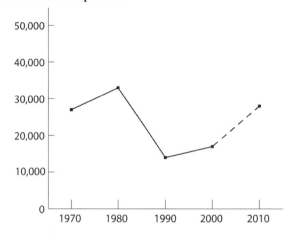

1. Numbers for 1970, 1980, 1990, and 2000 are taken from "Who Lives Downtown Today (And Are They Any Different from Downtowners of Thirty Years Ago)?" prepared for the Lincoln Institute of Land Planning by Eugenie L. Birch, May 2005.
2. Number for 2010 estimated as a result of data from agencies in each city.

LOS ANGELES

Los Angeles Downtown Area

1/2 inch = 1 mile. Source: Copyright 2002 ESRI; used with permission

Downtown Los Angeles has had a substantial number of residents for some time, but many of those were low-income minorities who depended upon a large stock of inexpensive housing close to bustling open-air markets and shops. However, urban renewal efforts in recent decades left many areas of the downtown in shambles, with entire blocks flattened and paved for parking lots. Even if someone wanted to make use of an older commercial building for a new use such as housing, he would encounter regulations and requirements from a myriad of city agencies.

According to Con Howe, former director of planning, all that changed in the late 1990s. "The city simply decided to get out of the way. We decided that regulations should encourage good development to occur, not make it more complicated," he says. The city adopted a series of reforms, including an adaptive reuse ordinance that made conversions of older buildings dramatically easier. Rather than requiring an onerous variance procedure, such alterations were allowed by right. Simple codes with considerable discretionary decision making were adopted. In subsequent years, scores of older, former office buildings—some built as recently as the '70s—have been converted to condominiums.

The conversion process allowed downtown to be recognized in the market as a desirable place to live. This has had the effect of encouraging new construction. Since the year 2000, according to Howe, 7,000 units have been completed and another 9,000 are permitted or under construction. Urban neighborhoods are emerging in what were previously empty blocks and buildings.

Los Angeles Downtown Resident Data

Income	Median Low: $6,250
	Median High: $25,721
Race and Ethnicity	White: 29.2%
	Black: 18.3%
	Asian: 16.9%
	Hispanic: 50.6%
Age	Under 18: 18%
	18-24: 11%
	25-34: 19%
	35-44: 17%
	45-64: 22%
	Over 65: 14%
Educational Attainment	H.S. Diploma: 47%
	Bachelor Degree: 15%
	Graduate Degree: 7%

Information for 2000. Source: "Who Lives Downtown Today (And Are They Any Different from Downtowners of Thirty Years Ago)?" prepared for the Lincoln Institute of Land Planning by Eugenie L. Birch, May 2005

Los Angeles Downtown Population

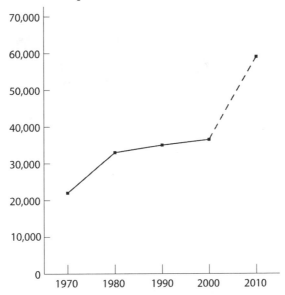

1. *Numbers for 1970, 1980, 1990, and 2000 are taken from "Who Lives Downtown Today (And Are They Any Different from Downtowners of Thirty Years Ago)?" prepared for the Lincoln Institute of Land Planning by Eugenie L. Birch, May 2005.*
2. *Number for 2010 estimated as a result of data from agencies in each city.*

LOWER MANHATTAN

Lower Manhattan Downtown Area

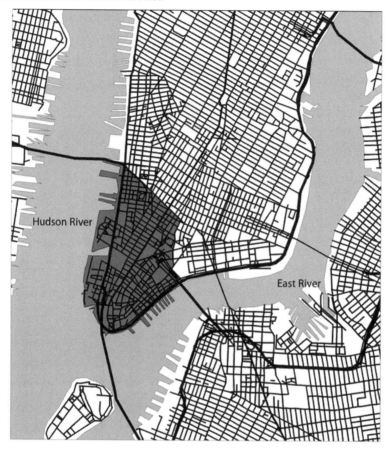

1/2 inch = 1 mile. Source: Copyright 2002 ESRI; used with permission

The area south of Houston Street began its transformation into an arts district in the early '70s, when the city began to allow artists to live in buildings still occupied by active industries and warehouses. Some pockets of dense urban housing gradually began to appear in blocks surrounding the financial district, although no sense of a true, multidimensional neighborhood was evident.

The development of Battery Park City in the 1980s, on the southwest tip of the island on landfill created by excavation for the World Trade Center, progressed beyond the initial phase of corporate office buildings to include substantial amounts of housing. In recent years, Tribeca (Triangle below Canal) has seen former industrial buildings converted into lofts, as well as new construction. A whole new neighborhood of mid- and high-rise housing has emerged, with shops, services, and an exquisite esplanade along the Hudson River.

Since then, many areas near Lower Manhattan have seen dramatic increases in housing, including Nolita (north of Little Italy) and even the formerly languishing Bowery. Clearly, Lower Manhattan has come to be seen as a viable, lively place to live—ironically, recalling the era in the mid-1800s when it held much of the city's housing stock.

Unfortunately, the tragic events of September 11, 2001, disrupted this trend. But with the passage of time, the further redevelopment and infilling of the district will reoccur.

Lower Manhattan Downtown Resident Data

Income	Median Low: $20,344
	Median High: $113,332
Race and Ethnicity	White: 44.7%
	Black: 5.7%
	Asian: 42.1%
	Hispanic: 11.4%
Age	Under 18: 15%
	18-24: 12%
	25-34: 20%
	35-44: 18%
	45-64: 23%
	Over 65: 13%
Educational Attainment	H.S. Diploma: 35%
	Bachelor Degree: 40%
	Graduate Degree: 18%

Information for 2000. Source: "Who Lives Downtown Today (And Are They Any Different from Downtowners of Thirty Years Ago)?" prepared for the Lincoln Institute of Land Planning by Eugenie L. Birch, May 2005

Lower Manhattan Downtown Population

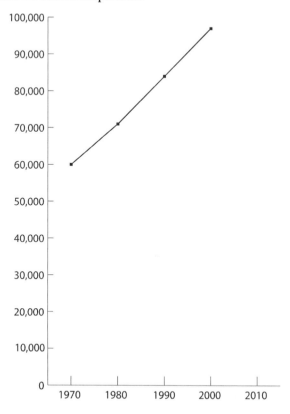

1. *Numbers for 1970, 1980, 1990, and 2000 are taken from "Who Lives Downtown Today (And Are They Any Different from Downtowners of Thirty Years Ago)?" prepared for the Lincoln Institute of Land Planning by Eugenie L. Birch, May 2005.*

MIAMI

Miami Downtown Area

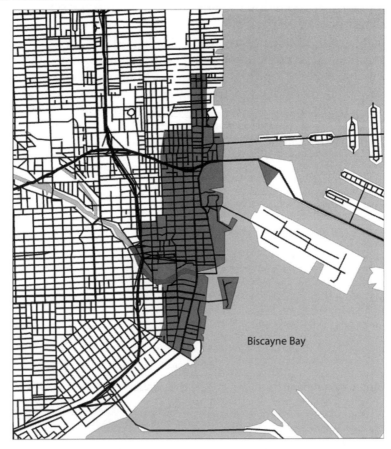

Biscayne Bay

1/2 inch = 1 mile. Source: Copyright 2002 ESRI; used with permission

Downtown Miami has been a pretty tough setting for some time. Older commercial buildings line tired streets in some sections, while in others, sleek new hotels and office towers rise up to create a sparkling skyline that is depicted in movies and television shows. But downtown was never really viewed as a place to live—until now.

Previous efforts to add new vitality, in the form of shopping areas like Bayside, a performing arts center, museums, and a stadium, may have altered that perception, and today numerous new residential projects are being built—many with stylish, neo-modern designs showcased in the national edition of the *New York Times*.

According to former Miami planning director Sergio Rodriguez, FAICP, who is now with University of Miami, the major public investments of a decade ago are paying off. Similarly, he notes that other nearby cities such as Coral Gables now have high-rise, high-density residential development in their downtowns. Rodriguez also observes that rail transit has had an impact, with new, dense mixed use developments occurring around rail stations such as Dadeland.

According to the city planning department, more than 3,000 units of housing have been built in downtown Miami since the year 2000. Another 9,000 are under construction and 17,000 are in the permitting process.

Miami Downtown Resident Data

Income	Median Low: $7,595
	Median High: $61,807
Race and Ethnicity	White: 64.7%
	Black: 27.6%
	Asian: 0.0%
	Hispanic: 49.4%
Age	Under 18: 16%
	18-24: 10%
	25-34: 22%
	35-44: 18%
	45-64: 22%
	Over 65: 12%
Educational Attainment	H.S. Diploma: 29%
	Bachelor Degree: 38%
	Graduate Degree: 20%

Information for 2000. Source: "Who Lives Downtown Today (And Are They Any Different from Downtowners of Thirty Years Ago)?" prepared for the Lincoln Institute of Land Planning by Eugenie L. Birch, May 2005

Miami Downtown Population

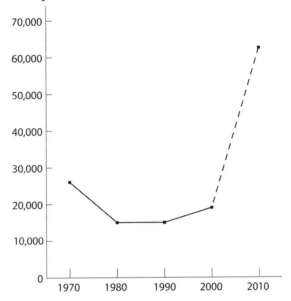

1. *Numbers for 1970, 1980, 1990, and 2000 are taken from "Who Lives Downtown Today (And Are They Any Different from Downtowners of Thirty Years Ago)?" prepared for the Lincoln Institute of Land Planning by Eugenie L. Birch, May 2005.*
2. *Number for 2010 estimated as a result of data from agencies in each city.*

MILWAUKEE

Milwaukee Downtown Area

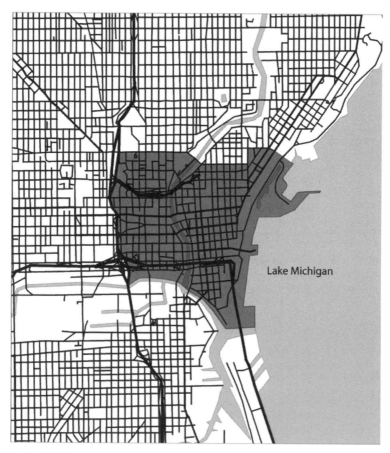

Lake Michigan

1/2 inch = 1 mile. Source: Copyright 2002 ESRI; used with permission

"The smartest thing that the city did was get out of the way," says Nancy Frank, chair of the Urban Planning department of the University of Wisconsin–Milwaukee. But she also asserts that several other actions are responsible for the resurgence of downtown living. For example, the city radically improved the streetscape in several districts.

The Third Ward received a complete makeover. Design firms and art galleries moved in, giving the area a distinct ambiance. The city worked with the Light Opera Company to find a venue in the district. And the Milwaukee Institute of Art located there.

Dense housing has been constructed on formerly vacant parcels on the site of a demolished 1980s-era freeway on the south side of downtown. There is enough density now to support a major grocery store and another is being planned. The Fifth Ward has many warehouses converted into lofts. The emerging Beerline B district along the river also has new housing.

Within the core, older office buildings are being converted to residential use, and on Library Hill, a 22-story residential project is under way. According to the Milwaukee Department of City Development, over 5,500 housing units have been completed, are being built, or have been announced within the downtown area since 2000.

Milwaukee Downtown Resident Data

Income	Median Low: $11,202
	Median High: $53,125
Race and Ethnicity	White: 70.7%
	Black: 22.1%
	Asian: 3.7%
	Hispanic: 3.0%
Age	Under 18: 7%
	18-24: 28%
	25-34: 27%
	35-44: 14%
	45-64: 16%
	Over 65: 9%
Educational Attainment	H.S. Diploma: 14%
	Bachelor Degree: 46%
	Graduate Degree: 16%

Information for 2000. Source: "Who Lives Downtown Today (And Are They Any Different from Downtowners of Thirty Years Ago)?" prepared for the Lincoln Institute of Land Planning by Eugenie L. Birch, May 2005

Milwaukee Downtown Population

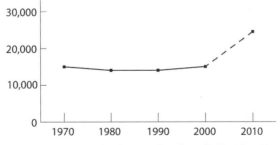

1. *Numbers for 1970, 1980, 1990, and 2000 are taken from "Who Lives Downtown Today (And Are They Any Different from Downtowners of Thirty Years Ago)?" prepared for the Lincoln Institute of Land Planning by Eugenie L. Birch, May 2005.*
2. *Number for 2010 estimated as a result of data from agencies in each city.*

PHILADELPHIA

Philadelphia Downtown Area

1/2 inch = 1 mile. Source: Copyright 2002 ESRI; used with permission

Richard Bartholomew, AICP, of the Philadelphia-based design firm Wallace Roberts & Todd, credits the City Center District Plan and tax credits with adding substantial numbers of new dwelling units to a downtown that has traditionally contained much housing. Today, the downtown has a population approaching 90,000. Some of this is due to the superb system of public transit which allows many households to live well without a car and the presence of the University of Pennsylvania campus, which has an almost seamless interface with downtown. The university has been a stabilizing influence on the areas surrounding it and has been careful to not create the "fortress" effect seen in many urban universities.

According to the city's website, since 1998, over 6,000 new residential units have been added, 84 percent of which involved conversions of buildings from other uses. Like other cities, Philadelphia has made extensive use of a 10-year tax abatement program to encourage new investment. At the end of 2005, another 4,000 units were under construction. The Central Philadelphia Development Commission expects another 7,200 units to be added over the next several years.

The website also notes that downtown home values have generally increased 20 to 30 percent in the last few years, with one neighborhood, Southwest City Center, increasing by 94 percent. Even so, housing in downtown Philadelphia is significantly less costly than that found in the downtowns of other major East Coast cities.

Philadelphia Downtown Resident Data

Income	Median Low: $8,349
	Median High: $87,027
Race and Ethnicity	White: 75.7%
	Black: 12.6%
	Asian: 8.0%
	Hispanic: 4.0%
Age	Under 18: 7%
	18-24: 15%
	25-34: 30%
	35-44: 15%
	45-64: 20%
	Over 65: 14%
Educational Attainment	H.S. Diploma: 10%
	Bachelor Degree: 67%
	Graduate Degree: 36%

Information for 2000. Source: "Who Lives Downtown Today (And Are They Any Different from Downtowners of Thirty Years Ago)?" prepared for the Lincoln Institute of Land Planning by Eugenie L. Birch, May 2005

Philadelphia Downtown Population

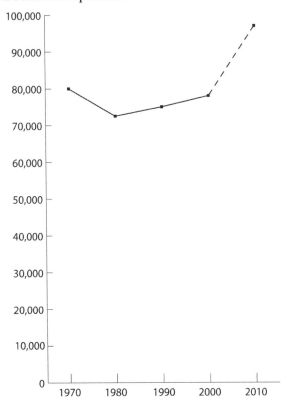

1. Numbers for 1970, 1980, 1990, and 2000 are taken from "Who Lives Downtown Today (And Are They Any Different from Downtowners of Thirty Years Ago)?" prepared for the Lincoln Institute of Land Planning by Eugenie L. Birch, May 2005.
2. Number for 2010 estimated as a result of data from agencies in each city.

PORTLAND

Portland Downtown Area

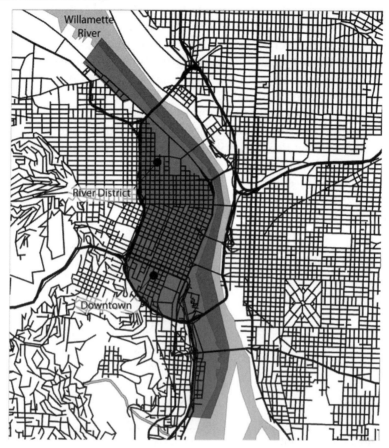

1/2 inch = 1 mile. Source: Copyright 2002 ESRI; used with permission

Portland, Oregon, began laying the groundwork for the emergence of downtown neighborhoods several decades ago. The removal of a freeway on the west side of the Willamette River and the installation of an expansive park in its place triggered a new interest in housing, with mid-rise, mixed use development occurring along the river at the south end of the park.

The addition of a bus transit mall, followed by an immensely popular light-rail network, and then—more recently—a streetcar, have given downtown a reputation for being highly accessible without the hassles of taking a car there.

The development of Pioneer Courthouse Square on the site of a former parking lot gave downtown a shared "living room." This hardscaped open space complemented the many park blocks that had been a long-standing feature of downtown. The presence of Portland State University on one edge of downtown has attracted new housing.

Finally, the conversion of the River District, an older warehousing and industrial district on the north side of downtown (now renamed the Pearl District), has established a large, new, and dense urban neighborhood filled with town houses, lofts, and mid- and high-rise residential buildings. Laced throughout the district are several fine parks and a number of mews lined with ground-related housing.

During this decade, several thousand new units were built in the downtown and the Pearl District, and several thousand more are in various stages of development.

Portland Downtown Resident Data

Income	Median Low: $8,179
	Median High: $45,779
Race and Ethnicity	White: 77.0%
	Black: 6.6%
	Asian: 8.3%
	Hispanic: 5.0%
Age	Under 18: 3%
	18-24: 20%
	25-34: 24%
	35-44: 17%
	45-64: 25%
	Over 65: 12%
Educational Attainment	H.S. Diploma: 13%
	Bachelor Degree: 36%
	Graduate Degree: 13%

Information for 2000. Source: "Who Lives Downtown Today (And Are They Any Different from Downtowners of Thirty Years Ago)?" prepared for the Lincoln Institute of Land Planning by Eugenie L. Birch, May 2005

Portland Downtown Population

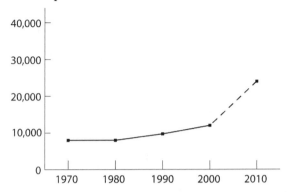

1. *Numbers for 1970, 1980, 1990, and 2000 are taken from "Who Lives Downtown Today (And Are They Any Different from Downtowners of Thirty Years Ago)?" prepared for the Lincoln Institute of Land Planning by Eugenie L. Birch, May 2005.*
2. *Number for 2010 estimated as a result of data from agencies in each city.*

SAN DIEGO

San Diego Downtown Area

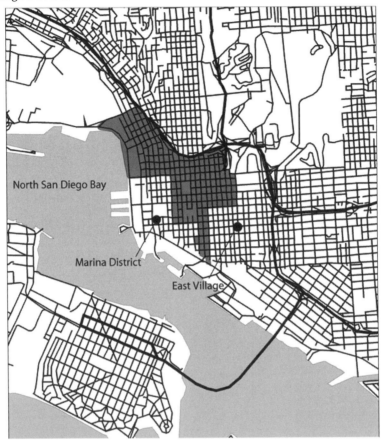

1/2 inch = 1 mile. Source: Copyright 2002 ESRI; used with permission

Michael Stepner, FAICP, served as city architect during a time when various initiatives helped lay the foundation for what today is an astonishing boom in downtown housing. Stepner credits Peter Wilson, who served as mayor between 1971 and 1984, for setting in motion many of those actions. For example, the Centre City Development Corp. has helped assemble land for many different types of projects that implemented a visionary downtown plan adopted in 1975.

The development of the Horton Plaza retail complex, the revitalization of the Gaslamp Quarter and the Marina District, and the addition of light rail established downtown as a desirable place. Several new and distinct neighborhoods have begun to emerge, including Columbia and the East Village. The city has been vigilant about ensuring the provision of below-market-rate housing with an innovative program of SRO buildings for service workers.

Eminent domain has been used to assemble property and provide public amenities. Tax Increment Financing is also a major tool. And the city has invested in significant public improvements to create identities for various districts. Finally, Stepner gives much credit to planner Max Schmidt for his persistent advocacy of downtown and as "the keeper of the flame."

According to Jason Luker of the Centre City Development Corp., which also monitors construction and permitting, almost 7,500 units were built in the first half of this decade in and near downtown. Another 3,900 units are under construction and 7,500 units are in the permitting process. In total, downtown San Diego will have almost 20,000 new apartments and condominiums during this decade.

San Diego Downtown Resident Data

Income	Median Low: $11,535
	Median High: $44,810
Race and Ethnicity	White: 66.4%
	Black: 11.9%
	Asian: 5.9%
	Hispanic: 24.3%
Age	Under 18: 7%
	18-24: 10%
	25-34: 22%
	35-44: 21%
	45-64: 26%
	Over 65: 14%
Educational Attainment	H.S. Diploma: 20%
	Bachelor Degree: 26%
	Graduate Degree: 9%

Information for 2000. Source: "Who Lives Downtown Today (And Are They Any Different from Downtowners of Thirty Years Ago)?" prepared for the Lincoln Institute of Land Planning by Eugenie L. Birch, May 2005

San Diego Downtown Population

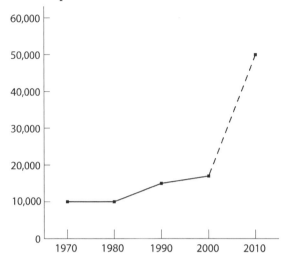

1. Numbers for 1970, 1980, 1990, and 2000 are taken from "Who Lives Downtown Today (And Are They Any Different from Downtowners of Thirty Years Ago)?" prepared for the Lincoln Institute of Land Planning by Eugenie L. Birch, May 2005.
2. Number for 2010 estimated as a result of data from agencies in each city.

SAN FRANCISCO

San Francisco Downtown Area

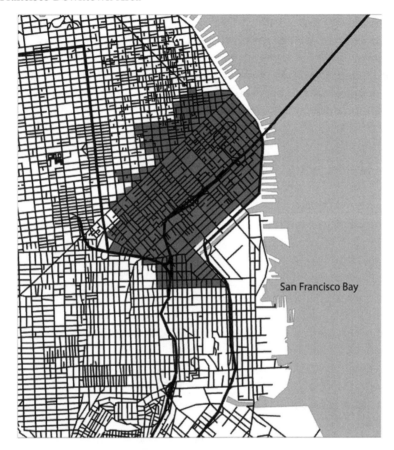

1/2 inch = 1 mile. Source: Copyright 2002 ESRI; used with permission

Dean Macris, FAICP, is once again San Francisco's planning director. He previously served in that capacity between 1980 and 1992, when the city put in place many programs and projects aimed at strengthening downtown. Since then entire districts within and near downtown have been transformed into new, mixed use neighborhoods.

Macris cites the Van Ness corridor as a dramatic example. Back in the '80s, property owners were clamoring for high-rise office zoning. The city instead insisted upon housing being the preferred use. In the ensuing years, thousands of new units have been built atop street-level retail.

The South Beach neighborhood has become a compact, highly walkable district filled with mid-rise housing within a stone's throw of the waterfront and the light rail along the Embarcadero. Rincon Hill was rezoned to encourage high-rise housing and a 50-story tower has recently been proposed. The district surrounding the Moscone Convention Center has matured, with housing for different incomes located close to the concentration of parks, museums, entertainment, and shops.

Amit Gosh, the city's planning manager, reports that more than 5,000 units of housing have been built in downtown since 2000. Another 5,000 to 6,000 are under construction and 25,000 more units are in the permitting process.

San Francisco Downtown Resident Data

Income	Median Low: $12,054
	Median High: $77,922
Race and Ethnicity	White: 46.7%
	Black: 9.8%
	Asian: 33.0%
	Hispanic: 11.7%
Age	Under 18: 8%
	18-24: 11%
	25-34: 23%
	35-44: 19%
	45-64: 26%
	Over 65: 14%
Educational Attainment	H.S. Diploma: 27%
	Bachelor Degree: 34%
	Graduate Degree: 12%

Information for 2000. Source: "Who Lives Downtown Today (And Are They Any Different from Downtowners of Thirty Years Ago)?" prepared for the Lincoln Institute of Land Planning by Eugenie L. Birch, May 2005

San Francisco Downtown Population

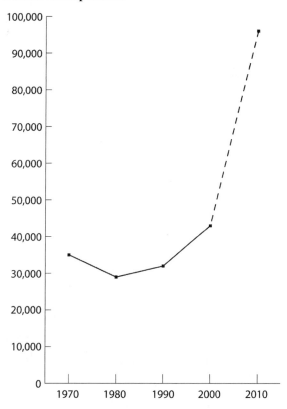

1. *Numbers for 1970, 1980, 1990, and 2000 are taken from "Lives Downtown Today (And Are They Any Different from Downtowners of Thirty Years Ago)?" prepared for the Lincoln Institute of Land Planning by Eugenie L. Birch, May 2005.*
2. *Number for 2010 estimated as a result of data from agencies in each city.*

SEATTLE

Seattle Downtown Area

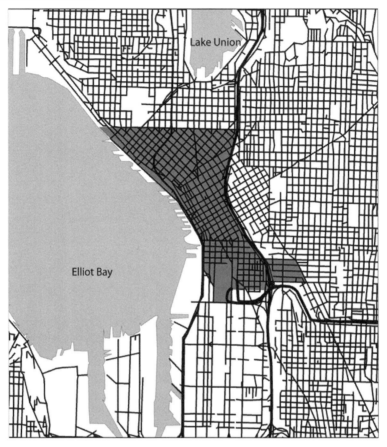

1/2 inch = 1 mile. Source: Copyright 2002 ESRI; used with permission

In the early decades of the 20th century, Seattle sluiced a huge piece of its dramatic topography called Denny Hill into nearby Elliott Bay and Lake Union. The intent was to allow for a northward expansion of the downtown. Trouble was, nothing much was built. For decades, scattered mid-rise apartment buildings were adrift in seas of asphalt parking lots that served as cheap daytime parking for downtown workers. A plan in the '70s did little to change that, despite its forward thinking about density and mixed use. The only new development came in the form of nondescript, suburban-style, speculative office buildings.

Several policy directions adopted in the 1980s resulted in more than 20,000 people now living downtown, most of them where the former Denny Hill was—a dense urban neighborhood now called Belltown after one of the original pioneering families of the mid-1800s. First, the city rezoned the district to dramatically diminish the potential for office development, instead weighting the regulations in favor of housing. Second, the city revised its building codes to allow a hybrid of construction types, including five floors of frame over one to two floors of concrete. This allowed a less expensive form of mid-rise construction that brought thousands of units to the market at price points affordable to many more people.

Finally, the city has fully embraced the state's Growth Management Act and designated downtown as a recipient of high-density, mixed use development. Taller buildings are now permitted, design criteria are aimed at ensuring quality and character, and fees are imposed on new development to provide for affordable housing. Nonprofit housing developers have been responsible for building many hundreds of units of low- and moderate-income housing throughout the downtown. And the transit agency has, for at least two decades, offered free service within the core, which has been a boon to retailers and restaurants.

According to John Skelton of the City of Seattle, over 5,000 units have been built since 2005, and another 5,000 are anticipated over the next several years.

Seattle Downtown Resident Data

Income	Median Low: $13,057
	Median High: $38,361
Race and Ethnicity	White: 65.2%
	Black: 11.5%
	Asian: 14.1%
	Hispanic: 4.3%
Age	Under 18: 5%
	18-24: 12%
	25-34: 24%
	35-44: 18%
	45-64: 26%
	Over 65: 15%
Educational Attainment	H.S. Diploma: 17%
	Bachelor Degree: 37%
	Graduate Degree: 13%

Information for 2000. Source: "Who Lives Downtown Today (And Are They Any Different from Downtowners of Thirty Years Ago)?" prepared for the Lincoln Institute of Land Planning by Eugenie L. Birch, May 2005

Seattle Downtown Population

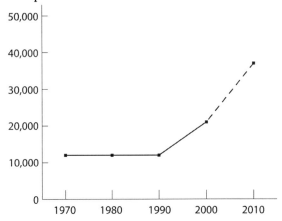

1. Numbers for 1970, 1980, 1990, and 2000 are taken from "Who Lives Downtown Today (And Are They Any Different from Downtowners of Thirty Years Ago)?" prepared for the Lincoln Institute of Land Planning by Eugenie L. Birch, May 2005.
2. Number for 2010 estimated as a result of data from agencies in each city.

Index

Questions for Discussion

How will aging baby boomers influence residential development in the next three decades?

It's long been a truism that young couples will abandon the city when they have children. Is this changing?

There is evidence that the popularity of in-town living is on the rise even in places without a long tradition of dense residential development, including cities in the western part of the country, where there is ample room for "horizontal" expansion. What is driving this change?

Much of the research on downtown living has focused on large cities, but there is anecdotal evidence that the trend is affecting inner-ring suburbs and smaller cities, too. Do you see evidence of this in your area?

Journalists have observed a correlation between high-density areas and liberal or Democratic voting patterns. Do you think this correlation exists? If it does, what are its long-term implications?

If we are nearing a peak in oil production, with attendant sky-high fuel prices, what will this mean for low-density, centerless suburbs?

As more people choose to live in high-density areas, what will this mean for public investments and services?

Some U.S. cities are attracting the relatively well-off (because of amenities) and the relatively poor (because of subsidized housing and services). Is it necessary for cities to find ways to accommodate the middle class? How can they do this?

What steps can cities take to encourage in-town living and higher density?

Once in-town living has been established in a city, what steps should the city take to ensure "inclusionary" practices?